new
kitchen
garden

new
kitchen
garden

organic gardening and cooking with herbs, vegetables, and fruit

ADAM CAPLIN

WITH **VEGETARIAN RECIPES**
BY **CELIA BROOKS BROWN**

photography **CAROLINE HUGHES**
food photography **WILLIAM SHAW**

RYLAND
PETERS
& SMALL
LONDON NEW YORK

First published in the USA in 2003
by Ryland Peters & Small
519 Broadway
5th Floor
New York, NY 10012
www.rylandpeters.com

10 9 8 7 6 5 4 3 2 1

Printed and bound in China

Senior designer Sally Powell
Senior editor Henrietta Heald
Location research manager Kate Brunt
Location researcher Sarah Hepworth
Production director Meryl Silbert
Art director Gabriella Le Grazie
Publishing director Alison Starling

Consultants Nick Robinson, David Grist
Proofreader Barry Gage
Indexer Alison Bravington

Library of Congress Cataloging-in-Publication Data
Caplin, Adam
   New kitchen garden : organic gardening and cooking with herbs,
vegetables, and fruit / by Adam Caplin & Celia Brooks Brown.
     p. cm.
ISBN 1-84172-224-3
   1. Organic gardening. 2. Herb gardening. 3. Vegetable gardening.
4. Fruit-culture. 5. Kitchen gardens. I. Brown, Celia Brooks. II. Title.

SB324.3 C36 2003
635'.0484–dc21   2002024942

vegetarian recipes for herbs, vegetables, and fruit

introduction

My first taste of gardening with edible plants came in the garden of my childhood, where there were few rules and few distinctions between what was edible and what was ornamental. Apple trees were trained along a raised walk underplanted with spurge and primroses and overhung by a huge ceanothus. Pear trees trained to form a candelabra stretched out from among evergreens in a border, and grapevines emerged from a chimney pot under a tree-form wisteria. Even the brussels sprouts earned a place near the perennials.

In the early days, being organic was not a priority, but as we grew up less spraying was done and more was left to nature. Plants such as comfrey threaded their way through a rose bed and soon

became a wonderful source of fertilizer, and companion plants abounded because of their beauty, encouraging beneficial insects to help control the pests.

The dahlia patch was transformed into a potato bed, and I remember my youthful excitement when digging the first crops, hoping not to spear any with my fork. Sometimes the results were disappointing but the successes made up for the failures. The taste of tiny new potatoes—freshly dug—left a lasting impression.

In today's smaller garden, where time and space are precious, there is no need to grow the perfect specimen or to win prizes for color and shape. Growing edibles is a source of satisfaction in itself, creating esthetic opportunities that would not exist if the separation between ornamentals and edibles persisted. I love to go out into my

small garden and cut roses and hellebores for the vase, evergreen pittosporums and buckthorn for foliage displays, and zucchini, tomatoes, and garlic for a ratatouille.

As the passion for growing edibles takes hold, you may want to transform more and more of your outdoor space, and perhaps to create a more dedicated kitchen garden area. Many gardens combine beauty with stimulation to the tastebuds, even where there are few pure ornamentals in sight.

I hope that this book inspires you to embark on the adventure of integrating edible plants into your flower borders, containers, and windowboxes, and gives you the confidence to experiment and to enjoy your own garden's harvest. The delicious and simple recipes on pages 104–35 are full of exciting ideas for using your garden produce to best effect.

kitchen garden basics

the appeal of organic gardening

Much of the pleasure of growing edibles lies in the thrill of eating a fresh tomato straight from the vine, biting into the sun-warmed flesh of a newly picked plum, or pulling and munching a carrot—without worrying about any artificial residues on the skins. Gardening with edibles heightens our sensitivity to the chemicals we introduce into our gardens.

Organic gardening dispenses with chemical sprays and artificial fertilizers—which means tolerating some pests and diseases and some superficial damage. Many insects are welcome visitors because they help reduce the number of predators that feed on plants. A pest's natural enemies move about seeking their specific targets. Ladybugs and their larvae have a wonderful appetite for aphids; hoverflies and lacewing larvae feed on these pests, too. The broad-spectrum chemicals

tend to be indiscriminate and destroy both predator and parasite—and it is usually the parasites that come back first. A mixed garden, where ornamental and edible plants live side by side, is ideal for gardening organically. The flowers of many ornamentals lure beneficial insects, which help reduce pests on nearby edibles. Good attractants include meadow foam, california poppies, marigolds, and calendula.

The most efficient form of organic pest control is healthy plants. A strong, resilient plant is far better at resisting the effects of an aphid attack than a weak plant. A well-nourished, well-watered plant is not only far stronger than a drying-out specimen but also—like a healthy immune system in humans—has a greater chemical resistance to attack. Making sure each plant gets the right soil, water, and light conditions is the

ABOVE, LEFT TO RIGHT **Ladybugs are among the best and most fascinating garden friends, with a hearty appetite for aphids. Flowers entice them into the mixed garden. Ducks are an effective slug control, but for most of us with urban gardens, keeping ducks must remain a fantasy. A good mixed organic garden has a natural balance of beneficial and parasitic insects that prevents a build-up of harmful pests.**

ABOVE RIGHT **The unique creased blue-gray foliage of Italian black cabbage (cavalo nero) is a lovely foil for flowering plants.**

RIGHT **Fennel is invaluable in a flower border, where its delicate filigree wands soften some of the more vivid garden colors.**

foundation for success in an organic garden. Improving the soil with organic matter can never hurt. Feeding the soil and soil organisms—rather than fertilizing the plants directly—usually helps create better conditions for plants to thrive. Some pests are less easy to accept in the new kitchen garden than others, and require harder work to overcome. Slugs and snails have plenty of natural predators—frogs, toads, hedgehogs, birds, and ducks can do much to control them. But, for most of us, it is worth trying to reduce the numbers of slugs and snails and protecting the crops, particularly at an early stage when they are most vulnerable. Slug pellets containing metaldehyde can harm other animals if eaten, and I prefer not to use them. Preparations containing aluminum sulfate are less harmful, but far less effective.

An organic method of controlling slugs—especially good in an area that you are about to plant—is provided by parasitic nematodes. The nematodes are supplied by mail order in the form of a powder that is watered into the soil from early spring; it works particularly well on

OPPOSITE, ABOVE **Green manure can be dug into the soil when it has stopped growing. Although a green manure can keep a bed occupied for a season, it is a very environmentally friendly way to produce a healthy soil.**

OPPOSITE, BELOW LEFT AND RIGHT **Phacelia is a quick-growing green manure that can revive a tired soil. Its long-lasting flowers attracts beneficial insects.**

THIS PAGE **Homemade compost has a crucial role in a healthy organic garden. As well as feeding plants and helping control disease, it can lighten heavy soils or help dry soils retain moisture in summer. The compost can be used around existing plants, thereby rejuvenating soil in the entire garden.**

subterranean slugs and lasts about six weeks. Other methods include slug and snail beer traps, copper tape for containers, crushed eggshells, gravel or soot around plants, and petroleum jelly mixed with salt around the outside of containers (under the leaf line). Vulnerable crops can be protected early in life with a plastic bottle cut in half, placed over them, and sunk into the soil as a mini cloche. Slugs and snails tend to hide in cool, shady, moist places during the day. The best way to catch them is to go out at night with a flashlight when they are emerging and pick them off plants.

Soil Healthy soil is the starting point for a healthy organic garden. The challenge is how to rejuvenate existing soil without bringing in heavy diggers and truckloads of topsoil. Good soil contains plenty of nutrients and organic matter, which helps retain moisture when it is dry and to improve drainage when it is wet. It has an incredibly complex ecosystem—

a handful of soil is said to contain more microorganisms than there are people on earth. Eighty percent of soil life is contained in the top 4in (10cm). The aim of soil conditioning is to improve and deepen this layer, which may be shallow in a tired, neglected garden.

Established trees and shrubs can look after themselves. But if you grow edibles in between, they will appreciate some help since many of them have relatively shallow roots. Some plants, such as Mediterranean herbs, actually thrive in poor soil. Always match the soil conditions to the plant. When doing a big job such as improving very poorly drained soil, separate the topsoil from the subsoil by digging it up and putting it in a heap—then, once you have dug some fine gravel and organic matter into the subsoil, put the topsoil back.

One of the most important ways of improving the soil and recycling is to make sure you have room for a compost pile, or to find a good source of organic matter such as well-rotted manure. I like to add a bit of manure to the compost pile, which helps accelerate decomposition. Finished compost can be applied in spring or early summer, adding a wheelbarrow full of well-rotted compost to every 50 sq ft (5 sq m). Dig the compost lightly into the topsoil. Take care when feeding the soil—too much manure can scorch the roots of new plants. Eventually you can use the organic matter as a mulch, and worms will do the rest. If you don't have space for a compost bin or pile, consider a worm bin for kitchen waste, which turns into nutrient-rich compost. If you have a bare patch of garden, a green manure such as hairy vetch or cereal rye, sown in late summer and then dug into the soil in spring, helps break up the soil and adds nutrients and organic matter.

Growing conditions Plant a sun-loving specimen in deep shade and it will grow leggy and pale in a vain attempt to get more sun. A shade-loving plant grown in full sun is likely to burn and shrivel. Edibles grown in unfavorable conditions tend to be less attractive and less productive than they should be. A pear in shade flowers weakly and carries more diseases

In a really sunny bed you can use a natural canopy to create dappled shade.

and fewer fruits than one grown in sun. The key to success is to get to know the sun patterns in your garden. In a small garden this is not as simple as assuming that south-facing means lots of sunshine and north-facing does not. Overhanging trees, large walls, or nearby buildings can make an enormous difference. My own south-facing terrace is very sunny in early spring until the neighbor's large tree comes into leaf. Observation through the year is the most effective way of identifying the reliably sunny and shady areas. In a really sunny bed you can use a natural canopy, such as a vine twisting round a pergola, to protect salad vegetables from the heat of the summer sun.

The most difficult situation for edibles is dense shade. If the shade is caused by trees or shrubs, they can be thinned or cut back to create more light. But plenty of edibles enjoy partial shade, including morello cherry, Victoria plum, blackberry, some of the leafy greens like chard, spinach, and lettuce, and herbs such as chervil, mint, sorrel, and bay.

In a windy place, taller growers such as climbing beans, cardoons, and artichokes can get blown around and damaged. It is often worth putting in a few larger wind-tolerant ornamental plants—evergreens and cotoneasters, or a fruit tree such as a damson plum—to act as a windbreak and create a sheltered area.

OPPOSITE, ABOVE **Trees help to give structure to a garden and can transform small beds by adding height. The shade of the canopy is a good place to plant leafy greens and salads, but they must be kept well watered.**

OPPOSITE, BELOW **Dappled shade from a trellis not only changes the growing environment but also creates shadow patterns on the ground. As the climbers grow up and thicken, the shade will become gradually denser.**

ABOVE **Shade offers some good opportunities to display dramatic foliage. This variegated pineapple mint, for example, provides a real spark of light in the dark. But only a limited range of edibles can be grown in a really shady garden.**

RIGHT **The dark zone at ground level may offer an opportunity to grow taller edibles. Runner beans thrive with their roots in the shade, emerging joyfully from the gloom. Another plant that appears to welcome the sun with open arms is tall-growing corn.**

a dedicated kitchen garden area

If you decide to dedicate an entire area of your gardening to growing edibles, you can enjoy the twin pleasures of beautiful borders and plenty of homegrown produce at most times of the year.

A successful kitchen garden combines productivity with beauty. It offers not only the promise of an abundant harvest above and below ground, but also the visual delight of leaf textures and shapes, drifts of filigree foliage, and powerful architectural shapes. There are practical considerations, too. Choose edibles you really like to eat. Grow things that are expensive in the shops as well as fruits and vegetables that are especially delicious when freshly picked. Traditional kitchen gardens are planted in rows for ease of cultivation, and this can look well ordered and calming even in a small garden. Different forms of lettuce—red, bright green, curly, oak-leaf—interspersed with carrots for feathery contrast, transform the rows into a tapestry of complementary foliage. In a small

ABOVE **Every dedicated kitchen garden needs a separate working area, but this can be hidden by, for example, a frame for climbers.**

ABOVE LEFT **An intensive kitchen garden is a step back in time, where the world is somehow more civilized and relaxed. But don't be fooled— there is more work to this type of garden than meets the eye.**

OPPOSITE **A ground cover of various varieties of lettuce set against a vertical backdrop of beans climbing up a frame in late spring provides a mouthwatering foretaste of the abundant harvest ahead.**

garden you can make full use of the space by succession planting and interplanting. Plan to plant the more tender sun-loving plants—tomatoes, zucchini, or eggplant—in the spaces left by early maturing broad beans. Plant quick growers, such as salad greens, under slow crops such as

ABOVE AND ABOVE LEFT **The most effective way to grow quantities of edibles is in simple rows. It is also one of the most esthetically pleasing arrangements, because it is historically familiar and most people feel happy with it. Growing purely decorative plants in this way would look strange.**

RIGHT **Informal plantings of edibles—with a few ornamentals mixed in—look natural and appropriate in a cottage-style garden.**

parsnips, leeks, and onions. In mild-winter areas, extend the season by planting some winter crops. Hide the rather tatty stems of brussels sprouts behind the exuberant foliage of chard. In a sunny corner of my garden, a drift of broad beans gave me a really good crop in the spring; after they were harvested, it became the perfect place for summer crops, including corn, 'Lollo Rossa' lettuce, tomatoes, zucchini, basil, marigolds, and a ground cover of arugula.

In a large border it is worth creating structure and height—both for impact and as a reference point for the rest of the planting. Add a teepee for climbers, a fruit tree, or a tall and dramatic plant. Walls provide opportunities to grow more climbers and fruit, whether single-stemmed cordons, fans, or espaliers.

When planting the border, you can have fun with the extraordinary choice of colors, shapes, and textures offered by edibles. An architectural silver-leaf artichoke, with its dramatic purple flowers, makes a great foil for the soft grays of sage, the dark berries of

a black currant and the purple pods of a snap bean, lifted by clumps of pale-green chives. If it is warm enough, some pots of eggplant round off a symphony of blues and purples. A teepee of runner beans at the back of a border sets off the lower-growing dwarf snap beans, spinach, carrots, onions, and shallots. A fig tree against a hot wall, surrounded by aromatic herbs such as rosemary, lavender, and thyme, and cooled by a haze of fennel, brings the Mediterranean to your garden. Fall raspberries with ruby chard, red-leaf beets, and low-growing 'Salad Bowl' make a red-hot scheme, with a line of leeks as a firebreak.

A low edging around the beds can bring coherence to the most informal scheme. Traditional boxwood is the neatest, but dwarf lavender is attractive and scented, while parsley makes a vibrant green frill, and alpine or wild strawberry a delicious fringe. Any small edible is worth considering. The fun of the kitchen garden is to let your imagination run wild, and above all to enjoy it.

LEFT **Even in the smallest of spaces a few edibles can help spice up the scene. The elegant bronze fennel adds height and form, while the thyme keeps the surrounding area fragrant.**

RIGHT **Zucchini, which like plenty of space, make good partners both for foliage plants and for flowers. A California poppy shows how beneficial flowers can also be attractive.**

FAR RIGHT **Fill some of the gaps in an established border with edibles instead of bedding plants. This tomato plant will provide a bit of color as well as delicious fresh tomatoes.**

adding edibles to an existing garden

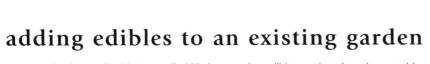

Anyone who has walked into a walled kitchen garden will know that there is something special about seeing edibles growing in a garden. It feels wholesome and mellow—perhaps the feeling of being a provider remains a fundamental part of the human psyche. Just watch the excitement when children discover that strawberries are not born in a pint basket and apples hang, unlabeled, from a tree.

A few years ago I wanted to introduce more edibles into my garden without major upheaval. The gaps under the golden-leaf black locust 'Frisia' could have been filled with pure ornamentals—but throwing string through a low branch and planting climbing snap beans gave me a wonderful display of flowers and a generous crop of beans.

The small raised bed that had been exclusively rockroses was a perfect place to introduce some Mediterranean herbs, such as rosemary, bay, thyme, and sage. The overgrown pittosporum was clipped into a tree form to provide space in the bed for the feathery fronds of bronze fennel. Pansies became even more beautiful when partnered with golden marjoram and *frais du bois*, a wild strawberry, mingled with geraniums; the combination created an attractive ground cover. Arugula looked like nature's gift in the border, with surprisingly jolly and delicious flowers, and blackberry's sparkling white flowers in spring brightened the shade under the sumac. The whole feeling of the garden changed. Integrating edibles into your existing garden—and transforming it from a purely ornamental garden into a new kitchen garden—can be both easy and rewarding. The unrivalled beauty of many edible plants creates a whole new palette for the gardener. A gap that might formerly have been filled with bedding plants becomes a perfect place for a compact tomato and purple basil; a space in the bed in front of a purple-leaf smoke bush might be filled with Italian black cabbage (cavolo nero) threaded

through with nasturtiums. A shady wall can become the support for a fan-trained morello cherry, and a pergola becomes the sturdy frame for the delicately cut leaves of an Oregon thornless blackberry.

There are some areas that are more difficult to manage. A well-established garden with few gaps will need some surgery—even the removal of some plants—to provide the necessary space. If the area you want to plant is close to greedy or bullying plants,

Growing edibles can be addictive. The transformation from a purely ornamental garden to a mixed garden frequently leads to more substantial changes.

LEFT **A magnificent acanthus flower and pulmonarias leave space for little else apart from the verticals in this ornamental corner. A wall of beans and a pier of grapes in leaf make an effective screen, which is transformed when heavy with fruit.**

ABOVE AND ABOVE LEFT **Tropical tree ferns make a surprising support for a mini cucumber; a single potato nonchalantly leans out of the raised bed. Squashes growing up a pyramid of canes add liveliness and height to a mixed border.**

it makes growing much more difficult because the edibles will need far more attention. You might consider installing a raised bed or placing large containers on the soil. Dense shade also limits the range of edibles that can be grown, particularly if it is under a sycamore, linden, or ash.

Even in the smallest spaces, herbs are an excellent starting point for growing edibles. Attractive and easy to cultivate, they also make elegant companions for other plants. Thyme, oregano, and marjoram create beautiful scenes when combined with the silver leaves of dusty miller, artemesia, or santolina, or when interrupted by tufts of chives or grasses. A rosemary can be planted beside a path so that its aroma melts into the air as you brush past it. The dusky-gray

Salvia officinalis creates a foil for other plants and becomes the star of the show when in glorious blue flower. The variegated form blends wonderfully with other herbs or creates a dramatic contrast with the purple *S. Purpurascens*. Chives and garlic chives are beautiful and resilient and make appealing edging plants, particularly near roses.

If a bit of height is required in a border, consider planting a Falstaff Red apple, which flowers so prolifically that it looks like a floral beacon in spring, then bears masses of apples throughout summer in advance of an abundant harvest in early fall. A simple teepee of canes with climbing beans, which are easy to grow, with leaves like soft green hearts, will provide at least four months of delicate flowers and

RIGHT **Zucchini, tomatoes, and corn dominate a bed that used to be purely ornamental. But I would make room in any garden for an agapanthus such as this one on the ground in a container.**

FAR RIGHT **A mature fruit tree can become a focal point. Growing a few ornamentals beneath it extends the season of interest.**

BELOW RIGHT **Growing tomatoes near a deep purple tradescantia emphasizes the delicate quality of their flowers.**

OPPOSITE, ABOVE **The large leaves of zucchini seem so welcoming and set up a beautiful contrast with the striking flowers of a sea holly.**

OPPOSITE, BELOW **The delicious amber tones of a viola 'Irish Molly' scramble through a golden marjoram. I love the pictures you can create by including edibles in your palette of plants and encouraging a little whimsy and a little luck.**

elegant fruit. In a larger border, the sculptural impact of angelica, with its huge heads of lime-green flowers, is magnificent. The globe artichoke, one of the finest vegetables, could also lay claim to be nominated as one of the finest ornamentals, with its powerful growth of silvered leaves and startling blue flower heads.

Squashes grown up a pyramid or along wires are among those plants that can raise the onlooker's spirits, with their beautiful joyful flowers, large floppy leaves and fruit that seems as if it could have come from another world. Rhubarb is an outstanding foliage plant that is virtually indestructible, and has enormous great spires of long-lasting creamy white flowers, thriving in partial shade.

In a sunny site in a border, a stand of corn resembles a giant ornamental grass. If it is planted near ornamentals such as agapanthus and alliums, the whole display looks stunning and harmonious. Simple round-headed cabbage interspersed with annual flowering grasses provide a contrast between the simple structure of the cabbage head and the filigree wands of the grass. An eggplant placed in a border with burgundy foliage of *Heuchera pilosissima* 'Plum Pudding' and the ferny haze of bronze fennel creates a sumptuous display, and golden orache, fresh young leaves of spinach, and wisps of dill make a subtle

The unrivaled beauty of many edible plants creates a whole new palette for the gardener to play with.

combination. Asparagus has delicate feathery foliage that makes a beautiful foil for many plants, as well as an appropriate background for ferns. In my garden, a mini cucumber uses a nearby tree fern as a living support, self-seeded nasturtiums forming a blazing orange carpet around and through raspberries.

I should end this section with a warning: growing edibles can be addictive. When you begin to transform your purely ornamental garden into a mixed garden, it frequently leads to more substantial changes. The shallots that looked beautiful in a small clump look even finer in a larger group; the temptation to plant one asparagus is tempered by the desire to be able to have a substantial crop—with the result that creating a more extensive area to grow edibles is a common part of the gardener's voyage of discovery.

RIGHT **Containers can be used to create space for edibles when the beds are densely planted. Here, purple and green basil and lettuce expand the mixed planting in the background.**

BELOW RIGHT **Even in the smallest of spaces you can grow fruiting treats. Strawberries are ideal for a small container and cascade over the rim like a waterfall.**

OPPOSITE, LEFT **Exotic colors and opportunities can be part of the thrill of the new kitchen garden. A red pepper looks glorious in a terra-cotta container and gives a colorful show in late summer.**

OPPOSITE, RIGHT **There are few more beautiful colors than this purple basil, which creates a harmonious display with the lilac shades of a simple painted can.**

pots, terraces, and roof gardens

Containers allow you to provide unique conditions for individual plants—so, if you don't have a good place for an edible in a bed, you may be able to grow it in a pot.

The most natural partners for small containers are herbs, especially those that thrive with some root restriction and are more tolerant of dry soils. Many of the Mediterranean herbs are ideal, especially if they have plenty of sun. The scent of thyme, lavender, or marjoram drifting in through the window adds an extra dimension to growing herbs on a windowsill. Parsley and sorrel are excellent plants for a container or a windowbox, as are the various types of mint, which may need to be split and repotted in fresh soil every couple of years.

Compact tomatoes will fruit prolifically as long as they are given an abundance of water. Chiles and peppers need the hottest place in the garden, with colors ranging from bright orange to black. Even larger-growing vegetables, such as corn and zucchini, can thrive in a container as long as it is big enough. I once filled a whole barrel with rotted manure and soil and had a prolific crop of gorgeous yellow flowers and zucchini tumbling over the side.

Container-grown edibles can be moved as the seasons change—so they benefit from being in the sunniest location through the year.

ABOVE LEFT **Chard and carrots promise crops above and below the soil. Edibles in containers seem to overflow wih goodness.**

ABOVE **A simple line of tomatoes in pots looks stylish and modern; they can produce a good crop as long as they are kept well watered and fed.**

ABOVE RIGHT **In many climates, citrus trees must be put indoors in winter. Growing them in a container makes it easier to move them around.**

LEFT, FROM LEFT TO RIGHT **The edibles in this children's garden will soon need potting up. Young spinach can be transplanted into a border or into other containers. Thyme creeps from a herb pot, and cut-leaf arugula grows happily in a hanging basket.**

Windowboxes make it possible to experiment with small plantings of herbs and vegetables. While it can be appealing to mix plants that require similar conditions, I prefer just one variety per container. If you combine them, one variety is usually more vigorous than the others and tends to take over. A mixture of purple, bush, and sweet basils looks great and provides an opportunity for artistry in the kitchen. A windowbox foaming with cut-and-come-again lettuce is a charming sight, and dwarf snap beans, which also have dainty flowers (delicious in salads), are a very attractive alternative to bedding plants.

Rooftop gardens often endure extreme conditions; they tend to be windier, sunnier and drier than an ordinary garden when it is hot, and wetter when it rains. By providing some protection from the wind, a convenient method of watering (such as a self-watering system) and containers with good drainage, you can grow some excellent Mediterannean herbs, vines, figs, and crops such as tomatoes that like lots of sun.

Recent developments have helped to produce rootstocks that limit the growth of apples, cherries and other fruit, making them ideal for containers. There is something strangely comforting about seeing fruiting cherry and apple trees on a balcony—or a lemon tree bursting with goodness after a summer vacation in the sun. Sitting under the shade of a fruiting grapevine on a roof garden, surrounded by the scent of figs, transports you magically to another place high in the mountains.

ABOVE **Seen from a worm's-eye view, lettuces thrive in the protected microclimate existing in the space between the cloches.**

ABOVE LEFT **Cloches provide just enough protection from spring frosts to start a few edibles early in the season. Fleece can prevent the tops of tender plants from being nipped by the cold and the wind.**

LEFT **A wooden octagonal greenhouse, cooled by the shade of parsnips left in to flower in their second year, provides the protection needed for an indoor grapevine.**

RIGHT **Visual flavors of decay and growth mingle as early tomatoes appreciate the light in the window of an old shed.**

FAR RIGHT, ABOVE AND BELOW **A small greenhouse gives the gardener some great opportunities—protecting tender plants, starting and growing plants throughout winter, and growing heat lovers in summer.**

The controlled conditions are ideal for introducing biological pest controls.

growing under cover

Giving plants a bit of cover—whether in the form of a gorgeous old bell jar or a simple cloche covered in plastic—helps protect tender crops, allows for earlier planting, and extends the season at the end of the year. It also speeds up plant growth and helps increase productivity. Lettuce, spinach, and carrots are among the vegetables that can be sown under a cloche in fall to mature in late spring.

Greenhouses If you have a greenhouse—that ultimate gardener's luxury—you can turn it into different rooms depending on the season. Early in the year it can act as a working area, where you can sow substantial quantities of seeds, using the shelving to house boxes of emerging seedlings. It enables the gardener to sow and harvest earlier, particularly in cold and temperate climates. I still remember the legions of young tomato plants—promising huge quantities of sauces and salads—grown by my father in his lovely little greenhouse.

As the season progresses, the seedlings are potted on and the greenhouse gets filled with pots of young plants eager to emerge into the open air. Later, when the youngsters have left their nest, the greenhouse can be taken over by tender edibles that thrive in the hothouse environment, and crop well with the benefit of extra heat, such as indoor tomatoes, melons, chiles, sweet peppers, and eggplant. The quality and yield of many of these are improved by being grown in a greenhouse, particularly because they are protected from the fluctuations of the weather.

Edibles that are tender in winter can be protected from late fall onwards—indeed, this is often the best way to grow citrus and passion fruit in a temperate climate. In a larger greenhouse a border can be used to plant fruit such as figs, peaches, apricots, nectarines, and vines, though mildew on vines can be a greater problem because of the still air.

Creating a natural balance in such an artificial environment is harder and there is less opportunity for wildlife to colonize. But the controlled conditions are ideal for introducing biological pest controls such as those for whitefly and red spider mite.

Cold frames Cold frames are excellent for providing the right environment for hardening off seedlings before transplanting them outside, and slightly taller cold frames can be used to protect some of the more tender crops such as chiles and melons, with their lids removed as the season warms up, to allow the plants to mature. The wooden lean-to and free-standing cold frames are particularly evocative and appropriate in a kitchen garden.

planning the year

There are plenty of tasks to be carried out in the new kitchen garden in the different seasons. Keep in mind that the timetable will vary depending on your location. For example, gardeners in mild-winter areas will be able to grow more edibles in spring and fall. To learn more about the best planting times in your area, contact your county cooperative extension service.

OPPOSITE, LEFT TO RIGHT **Put in place for the summer rush, these strings will soon be obscured by foliage, flowers, and beans. You hardly need any reminders to pick the fruit of your labor; if you don't, others will. Fall and winter mean compost time.**

Winter

A relatively quiet time in the kitchen garden.

- Tidy up the garden.
- In heavy soils dig in plenty of organic matter, but try to keep off the soil if it is very wet.
- Note areas with bad winter drainage; this may need to be improved.
- Prune apples, pears, quinces, currants, and gooseberry bushes, and prune grapevines to create a framework.
- Plant bare-root fruit trees and berries when not too cold.
- Check stakes on young fruit trees.
- Remove any diseased fruit or vegetables in store.
- Order from catalogs.
- Wash pots and seed trays for sowing.
- Continue to harvest root vegetables, leeks, and winter brassicas.
- In late winter sow early vegetable crops in greenhouse and cloches as appropriate.
- Prune fall-fruiting raspberries in late winter.

Early to mid spring

Plants are beginning to grow; most gardeners are reviving, too.

- Keep on top of the weeding with regular hoeing through the season.
- Give the soil around established plants a top dressing of manure or compost, and dig in lightly with a fork.
- Protect containers from slugs and snails with copper tape.
- Apply nematodes to control slugs, and set up slug and snail traps.
- Sow early vegetables and herbs in greenhouse or under cloches; sow outside if the soil is warm enough.
- Plant potatoes and onions as the soil warms up.
- Plant perennial vegetables, such as artichoke and asparagus.
- Start to buy seedlings from retailers and catalogs.

- Start to buy herbs.
- Clean up herbs in containers; give them a top dressing of fresh soil, or repot.
- Divide perennial herbs such as chives, mint, tarragon, and sorrel.
- Protect early flowering fruit blossom from frost with fabric row covers.
- Protect peach while in bud from rain with plastic tarp.
- Build structures for climbing beans.

Mid to late spring

As the weather improves, it is time to get the garden into high gear.

- Continue to sow and plant hardy vegetables and herbs outside, and sow and plant companion plants.
- Sow tender vegetables such as snap beans and zucchini under cover or cloche. Plant outside when all danger of frost has passed.
- Harden off and plant early crops sown inside.
- Continue slug and snail hunting.
- Start "hilling" potatoes. (Mound the soil around the base of the plant.)
- Start fertilizing plants in pots.
- Begin fertilizing established plants; give fruit trees and bushes a feed, and mulch to help to conserve moisture and inhibit weeds.
- Start planting herb containers; buy tender herbs.

Early to mid summer

A busy time when everything is growing strongly.

- Make sure that watering is thorough, allowing the water to soak into the ground.
- Continue to sow and plant vegetables and herbs.
- Start planting out tender vegetables such as tomatoes, peppers, and eggplant.
- Transplant winter crops such as leeks into the garden.

Even in summer—when the big task to enjoy the garden bounty—
it pays to do practical things such as sowing green manures.

- Prune dead and diseased wood from plums and cherries.
- Remove some fruit from tree if biennial bearing.
- Protect ripening fruit from birds with netting.

Mid to late summer

For most of us, the big job is to consume what we have been growing—but it is also worth thinking ahead.

- Harvest lots of fresh vegetables and keep on picking herbs.
- Sow green manures.
- Sow overwintering vegetables and winter salad crops.
- Cut back lavenders after flowering.
- Prune new growth on apples and pears to three to four buds from the old growth.
- Prune vines to three or four leaves after fruiting.
- Cut out fruited canes of summer raspberries and tie in new ones.
- Cut back old wood from black currants.

Fall

A relaxed time, with plenty to do and plenty to consume from the garden. Good time to make compost ready for the following season.

- In early fall make sure you have plenty of room in the compost bin.
- Plant garlic; sow broad beans.
- Sow winter salad crops.
- Start harvesting root vegetables.
- Remove fruited shoots from blackberries.
- Plant hardy perennial herbs and give the garden a clean-up.
- Remove annuals and compost them.
- Protect tender plants in containers from the cold and excess damp. Bring in citrus fruits.
- Water containers only when dry.
- Order seed catalogs.
- Review the season, noting successess and failures, and any gluts or shortages, to help determine the following season's numbers.

organic gardening with
herbs, vegetables, and fruit

When you look at a colorful seed rack or a thousand small pots of herbs, you might deduce that all herbs are small plants and that you could simply pack them in when planting. But, although there are thymes

herbs

and chamomiles that grow no higher than a carpet, there is also angelica that in its second season can become a tall, competitive bully and bay trees that can become the dominant feature of a garden. Some are annuals and have completed their lifecycle when they seed, while others last for decades. Many, including sage and rosemary, seem to be in their prime for about five years, when for no reason they give up the will to live. Even when dealing with such a diverse group, there are common techniques that will help the kitchen gardener to have a more fulfilling garden.

herb basics

Most annual herbs can be grown successfully from seed, and there is plenty of choice in garden centers and mail-order catalogs, including an expanding range of organic seed. If you are planning to start sowing in early spring, when the weather is too cold or unreliable to plant outside, use an indoor room or a greenhouse, if you have one. This is particularly important for herbs such as basil that require warm conditions.

Seed sowing All you need to sow herb seeds is a pot or small propagator and ready-made seed-starting soil. Always use a pot with good drainage and sow a few seeds into pre-moistened soil, leaving 2 hours between watering and sowing to allow excess water to drain off. Seedlings raised under cover should be pricked out into larger pots, then hardened off when all danger of frost has passed by putting them into a sheltered spot, and moving them in on a cold night, or planting them outside under a cloche. Slightly later, when the ground has warmed up, seed can be sown directly into the ground. The key is to prepare the soil by removing all weeds and creating a fine soil texture. Start by removing stones and breaking up soil lumps with a rake in a large area, or a trowel in a small area. Scattering a bit of seed-starting soil onto the surface provides an even better basis for sowing. Make sure the area is well watered and follow the instructions about planting depth. In a heavy soil, cover seed with fine moist soil and label immediately.

Ready-grown herbs Introducing ready-grown herbs into a garden is a good way to get started, particularly if you need only a few plants. There is a great range available. Some look almost impossibly glossy and perky early in the season; they have been grown in ideal conditions, under cover in a greenhouse with ventilation and disease control, so the shock of being moved into a garden with all nature's imperfections or even into a house can check their growth. This is a particular problem if you buy early in the season when forced plants such as basil and tarragon have soft and

sensitive growth. Keep them indoors until danger of cold has gone. Similarly, avoid plants with unnaturally large leaves and floppy stems, indicating that they may have been grown under cover for too long.

When buying perennials such as sage, lavender, rosemary, and bay, look for bushy well-branched plants rather than tall leggy ones. A compact bush will grow into a stronger and better balanced plant. Try to avoid plants with roots forcing their way out of the bottom of the pot—these have become potbound after being left hanging around for too long. For flowering herbs such as lavender, it is often worth waiting to buy them when in flower because the colors on the label can be a bit misleading.

Soil Most herbs dislike waterlogged roots and require a well-drained soil. In a poorly drained soil, dig a hole bigger than the pot and mix some sand or gravel into the subsoil. In a garden that remains constantly

OPPOSITE, LEFT **Chervil is a lovely addition to salads and other dishes, and is hard to buy fresh in supermarkets. Small pots like this one are easy to relocate—if you go away, move them into the shade to prevent drying out.**

OPPOSITE, RIGHT **If mint is allowed to grow freely in a border, it quickly becomes invasive. Growing it in a container helps to limit the spread.**

LEFT **When planting a container, particularly for herbs such as sage that need good drainage, put a layer of pot shards in the base.**

ABOVE **Plant the herbs so that they end up at the correct level. The eventual height of the soil should be about ½ in (1 cm) below the rim of the container.**

RIGHT **For instant effect, grow small herbs together, then replant them separately when larger.**

SOWING SEEDS IN A TRAY

RIGHT **Use a fine seed-starting mix, which is just the right consistency and fertility for germinating seeds. The soil should be gently firmed down before seeding.**

FAR RIGHT **Water the soil well, and make sure you give it a good drenching using a watering can with a fine rose on it. If the soil is allowed to dry out, it can be very difficult to rewet.**

BELOW, LEFT TO RIGHT **Sow the seed by gently tapping the packet as you move it across the surface of the soil. If some of the seeds end up closely grouped, don't worry – even experts find it difficult to spread them evenly. Spread a small layer of seed compost over the seeds, rubbing it between your hands to break up any clumps; alternatively, use a small sieve, which works just as well. Cover the tray with cling film or a piece of clear plastic to create a humid atmosphere; remove this as soon as the seed has germinated. Small, inexpensive propagators with plastic tops are available, and—for the genuine enthusiast—more sophisticated ones with bottom heat.**

IMPROVING DRAINAGE

ABOVE, LEFT TO RIGHT, AND RIGHT **Soils that are poorly drained may look perfectly all right during summer, but they can easily become waterlogged after rain. Many herbs, particularly those that are native to the Mediterranean, need excellent drainage, and can suffer if their roots are left standing in water. To help improve drainage in an area of the garden where you intend to plant a herb, dig in plenty of sand or fine gravel and mix it with the soil at the base of the planting hole. Plant the herb—in this case, a variegated sage—and mix some of the gravel with the soil that will be used to fill in the hole. When the herb is in place, scatter some gravel around the base of the plant. In a garden that does not drain well, a more radical solution might be necessary, such as installing drainage tile or gardening in a raised bed.**

moist, more extreme and back-breaking solutions are required—such as digging in plenty of organic matter into both the topsoil and subsoil and breaking up the clay. The best solution may be to build a raised bed, which not only improves the drainage but becomes a garden feature. In most soils, you can plant out by digging a bigger hole than the pot, and adding garden compost mixed with bonemeal. Gently tease the rootball to get some of the roots to face the new soil.

Feeding and pruning Many herbs grow happily in a garden with little feeding—they often get more than enough help from the yearly feast of homemade compost and manure. Indeed, many herbs grown in a less nutritious environment actually taste better. If a feed is needed, a dressing of compost or seaweed meal is excellent. Liquid seaweed is a pick-me-up for a starving plant and great for herbs in pots. Few herbs need formal pruning, especially since regular cropping tends to keep the plant compact and encourages new growth. A rosemary left unpicked often becomes tall and woody, whereas one that is regularly harvested can be a lush bush of fresh green growth. Thyme and lavender appreciate a haircut after flowering.

Container-grown herbs Herbs are ideal for growing in containers, providing you chose the pot to suit the plant and the right soil to provide good drainage, nutrients, and firm anchorage. Potting soil is excellent, although it is worth adding a bit of sand or fine gravel to make sure that drainage is adequate. Peat-based multipurpose composts are the easiest to use and give good early results, but the soil soon runs out of nutrients and can be very hard to rewet if it dries out. There are plenty of peat-free alternatives, which are improving all the time.

PINCHING OUT
Nipping buds and flowers off a basil plant helps to keep it producing leaves and looking bushy rather than leggy. Use the buds as you would the leaves.

39

herbs

Herbs are among the most beautiful and most important of all the edibles—important because only a small quantity of a herb can make a dramatic difference to a dish. Home-grown tarragon can flavor a whole fish, sorrel opens up wonderful new opportunities with soups, and basil fills the air with Mediterranean memories. Many of the common culinary herbs are simple to grow.

Allium schoenoprasum. **Chives**. Perennial. With their purple drumstick flowers and fresh lively foliage, chives make gorgeous edgings for beds and spot plantings. They grow well in containers. They also combine well with many other herbs such as sage and thyme or as fillers in a border. Plant in sun or light shade. Once a clump of chives has become well established, it can be dug up in the fall and teased apart to make fresh new clumps. Garlic chives (*A. tuberosum*) are larger with balls of fragrant white flowers.

Anethum graveolens. **Dill**. Annual. Dill has feathery leaves and umbels of yellow flowers and is a worthy candidate for introducing to a flower border or growing in containers outside. The flowers are wonderful for attracting hoverflies, whose larvae feed on aphids. Plant indoors in spring or outside in summer. Dill thrives in a poorish, well-drained soil in a sunny position. Snip off leaves regularly to keep the plant in shape.

Angelica archangelica. **Angelica**. Biennial. Angelica is among the most spectacular of architectural plants and can be used to create a wonderful impact at the back of a border. Growing up to 8ft (2.5m) in height, it has fresh lime-colored leaves and great umbels of pale-green flowers. Choose a sunny site with rich, moist soil; sow the seeds in fall or spring—right where they are to grow. Tolerates a little shade and self-seeds freely.

ABOVE AND LEFT **The exquisite pale-green buds and flowers of angelica are reminiscent of cottage gardens. Angelica looks majestic in a large border—it has an architectural magnificence that dominates, while being modest enough to mix well with other plants.**

OPPOSITE, ABOVE **Dill has a delicate filigree leaf that looks good in this container, and mixes easily with most garden plants.**

OPPOSITE, BELOW **A clump of chives in a border looks full of enthusiasm and life before it bursts into full splendor. Chive flowers are not only beautiful in full bloom but are also exquisite in bud.**

41

Anthriscus cerefolium. **Chervil**. Annual. Chervil has a parsley-like flavor with hints of anise that adds spiciness to salads and cooked dishes. It resembles a small-growing fine-leaved cow parsley with rather more delicate light green leaves. Chervil is evocative of the countryside when dancing in a breeze and looks particularly appropriate in an informal planting. Sow seeds in spring or fall in light soil outside in semi-shade. In mild-winter areas, the last sowing will grow on through winter under cloches for fresh harvests. Given a bit of shade from the hot sun, chervil grows well; in hot, dry conditions it tends to go to seed.

Artemisia dracunculus. **Tarragon**. Perennial. For dishes *à l'estragon*, the only tarragon worth growing is the French variety. The herb grows well in a container, which can be given protection in winter. Although tarragon is a rather insignificant-looking plant, its flavor when freshly cut is wonderful when compared with what you can find in a supermarket. Tarragon can be grown under cover in winter, but tarragon picked in winter is more watery than the summer-picked herb and has less flavor. Buy a small plant and pot it in well-drained soil. It needs regular watering but hates having wet roots. Pick off the flowers and harvest leaves as you need them. Overwinter in a frost-free place or protect with garden fabric or mulch.

Borago officinalis. **Borage**. Annual. Borage has one of the most startling blue flowers of any plant, and combined with its soft gray-green foliage is valuable in a large border. There is also an attractive white form. Lovely with roses, or with fruit trees and with many perennials. Scatter seed in a sunny spot from spring or plant where you want it to flower. It can look effective as a wildish planting in containers. Borage draws beneficial insects to the garden. Chop up the leaves and use the flowers for a cucumber flavor in salads or cold drinks. Pimm's is the classic.

Chamaemelum nobile. **Chamomile**. Evergreen perennial. The flowering Roman chamomile is an attractive, sweetly scented plant that looks good in an informal setting. Sow under cover in fall or spring and plant out in a sunny site to roam in the border with its daisylike flowers that can be made into tea. To make a chamomile lawn or seat buy small plants of the non-flowering C. 'Treneague' and make sure the soil is very well drained. With frequent use, both the seat and lawn tend to get a little weedy and bare, but the scent is delicious.

ABOVE **Chamomile provides a fine head of hair for this container. The soil must be well drained to allow the herb to thrive.**

LEFT **Non-flowering chamomile makes an interesting lawn or seat, and the soft cushiony foliage has a sweet scent.**

ABOVE LEFT AND FAR LEFT **Borage has delightful flowers—the white form is very pure, while the color intensity seen in traditional blue borage makes the herb worth growing for its flowers alone.**

OPPOSITE **Tarragon is well suited to being grown in a pot because it can be given protection in winter. Freshly picked tarragon has a far better flavor than the dried herb.**

43

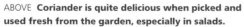

ABOVE **Coriander is quite delicious when picked and used fresh from the garden, especially in salads.**

ABOVE RIGHT AND FAR RIGHT **Fennel has delicate foliage that grows like a spray of mist. The bronze form is particularly striking in a garden.**

OPPOSITE, LEFT **Bay is a relatively hardy evergreen that produces copious quantities of aromatic leaves. The best flavor comes from plants that are not too well fed.**

OPPOSITE, CENTER ABOVE AND BELOW **Lavender has a long season of interest as well as fragrant foliage and flowers.**

OPPOSITE, RIGHT ABOVE AND BELOW *Lavandula stoechas* **and its many forms have exquisite flowers and a slightly stronger fragrance than traditional lavenders. Some varieties are tender, so it is worth checking to make sure they are hardy in your area.**

Coriandrum sativum. **Coriander (Cilantro)**. Annual. Fresh coriander has a wonderful flavor. The plant is not very ornamental, and can look a bit sulky if waterlogged. Sow plenty of coriander in fall or from early spring through to summer outside. Grows quite well in a pot. Coriander should be planted where you intend it to stay since moving it will make it bolt. It grows best in well-drained soil in a sunny location. The seeds are also edible and have a spicy flavor. For leaf production, pinch out the tops to delay flowering or plant a variety selected for leaf production. Coriander used in cooking is known as cilantro.

Foeniculum vulgare. **Fennel**. Perennial. Fennel is a superb plant for a kitchen garden. It is tall, feathery, elegant and bright green, and adds grace to the border. There is a striking bronze form, 'Purpureum', which looks particularly effective when planted with grays and silvers. Buy young plants or sow seed in spring in fertile, well-drained soil in a sunny location after the danger of frost has passed. Harvest the anise-flavored leaves through summer and the seeds in fall. Best in the garden but also good in large containers. The flowers attract hoverflies, which help to control aphids, and beneficial parasitic wasps. But new fennel growth seems to be a favourite with slugs and snails.

Laurus nobilis. **Bay**. Perennial evergreen in mild-winter areas. Bay trees are elegant aromatics that respond well to being clipped into architectural shapes. Bay makes a great foil for many ornamentals. It is surprisingly good in shade. Prefers well-drained soil and protection from cold easterly winds. Good in pots, but roots need protection in really cold winters. Susceptible

to scale insect, which can be cleaned off with warm soapy water. Bay sucker causes leaves to curl up; affected leaves should be picked off and burned.

Lavandula. **Lavender**. Perennial evergreen. Lavender has silvery leaves, beautiful flowers and a wonderful scent. The flowers come in every shade of blue and violet, as well as white. The flowers of French lavender, *L. stoechas*, have engaging 'ears'; check its hardiness in your area. Lavender can be used for evergreen edging or hedging—different types vary in height from 1ft (30cm) to over 3ft (1m). Grow in full sun in free-draining soil. Trim back close to the old wood after flowering.

RIGHT AND FAR RIGHT **The vibrant leaves of variegated pineapple mint bring sparkle to a border. Most mints have restful foliage. I find mints indispensable in my garden for making refreshing teas.**

OPPOSITE, ABOVE LEFT **Mints can grow well in very restricted spaces, but, although they tolerate shade, planting them in the sun produces a better flavor.**

OPPOSITE, ABOVE CENTER AND RIGHT **Its beautiful foliage makes purple-leaf basil an ornamental treasure. This is among the many basils that are ideal for containers. I always grow several basil plants so that each can have a short break from my greedy fingers.**

BELOW **Lovage has a relaxed country character, particularly in spring and early summer, when it is a more manageable size.**

OPPOSITE, BELOW **Golden marjoram creates a tight-headed mound that looks impressive in both formal and informal settings.**

Levisticum officinale. **Lovage**. Perennial. Lovage grows to a height of 5ft (1.5m) and half as much across after three years. It has giant hollow stems, fresh green divided leaves surmounted by tiny yellow flowers, and a celery-like scent. Grow lovage in your garden only if you have plenty of space. It combines well with other tall herbs such as angelica and fennel. The stems can be blanched and eaten, and the leaves are used to enrich soups, stocks and stews. Sow bought seed in spring or fresh seed in fall in moist soil. The herb thrives in sun or partial shade. Established clumps can be divided in early spring or fall.

Mentha. **Mint**. There is a dazzling selection of mints with all sorts of flavors, including pineapple and chocolate. Among the most useful are *M. spicata*, the common garden mint, and *M. suaveolens*, apple mint, which is similar with fruity overtones. Newly picked leaves are refreshing and light, and mint tea is a relaxing, healthy and delicious drink. Mints are great colonizers, so their invasive roots need to be curtailed in a container or a bottomless bucket in the garden. Buy mint as a young plant and position in sun or shade. Lift container every couple of years, split roots and fill with fresh soil. Mint rust, a tiny brown spotting on the leaves, is difficult to cure, so affected leaves should be picked off and burned as soon as they appear. Slugs and snails adore young mint foliage.

Ocimum basilicum. **Basil**. Annual. Basil is a first-class candidate for a pot on a sunny windowsill. Sow indoors from spring to early summer and put young plants outside after frosts in a sheltered sunny corner in well-drained soil. Pinch out leaves and flowers to keep plant compact. Bush basil, with smaller leaves, is a neat plant, excellent for growing in a pot, but has less flavor than the floppier sweet basil. Grow plenty of basil so that you always have enough to cook with. There are also purple and ruffled types—which are highly ornamental, though slightly more temperamental—and sacred basil, which is great in Thai recipes. Basil is often grown near tomatoes to keep the pests off, but in a bed it is very susceptible to slugs. If you are buying plants early in the season, bear in mind that most basil will be greenhouse grown and will dislike being moved into cooler conditions

Origanum spp. **Oregano** and **marjoram**. Oregano and marjoram are exceedingly decorative plants. The best for flavor is *O. marjorana*, or sweet marjoram, a half-hardy with downy, round, highly aromatic leaves and tiny white flowers in late summer. It springs easily from seed and grows to only 1ft (30cm), which makes it a good plant for a windowsill as well as outside. Pot marjoram, *O. onites*, is a small hardy shrub that has pink or purple flowers in late summer and the aromatic leaves are good for cooking. The golden 'Aureum' has lovely golden leaves and looks wonderful contrasted with purple sage. 'County Cream', a variegated form, is slightly less hardy. Oregano, *O. vulgare*, is hardy and good at attracting bees and butterflies. Oregano and marjoram like plenty of sun and well-drained soil. They blend well with silver leaves and are excellent edging plants. They all grow well in containers.

Petroselinum crispum. **Parsley**. Biennial, though often grown as annual. Curly-leaf parsley is the most decorative, in the garden as well as on the plate. The fresh green growth is full of enthusiasm in spring, though it is a greedy plant and can look a bit tired by the summer. Curly-leaf parsley needs a fertile well-drained soil that holds moisture well. It is lovely as an edging to a small bed, or in quite large pots. The flat-leaf parsley is less ornamental but has a better flavor. Parsley seed can take 4–6 weeks to germinate, but will do so much more quickly in a heated propagator. Parsley is vulnerable early in the season to slugs and snails.

Rosmarinus officinalis. **Rosemary**. Perennial. Rosemary is a evergreen shrub in mild-winter areas valuable for its architectural qualities as well as its aromatic culinary leaves and startling display of flowers. Rosemarys are easy to grow and worth planting near a door or path where they are likely to be brushed against. They grow well in containers in well-drained soil. 'Miss Jessopp's Upright' makes a lovely hedge, and the low-sprawling 'Severn Sea' makes waves of green that cascade downwards. 'Benenden Blue,' with light blue flowers, is particularly good in a tub. Colors range through all the blues to pinks and white. Rosemary needs plenty of sunshine, shelter, and good drainage.

Rumex acetosa. **Sorrel**. Perennial. Sorrel—a classic ingredient of French cooking—has a tangy lemon flavor that is delicious in soups, omelets, and salads. Broad-leaf sorrel grows well in partial shade and is excellent in containers. The fresh new leaves are a gentle green. Buckler-leaf sorrel (*R. scutatus*) has smaller leaves that are good in salads and makes a useful ground-cover plant. Sow seed outside in spring in sun or partial shade. Remove the flower spikes to encourage leaf production.

Salvia officinalis. **Sage**. Perennial. With its soft, evergreen, furry leaves, sage is a lovely ornamental, looking quite at home even in the showiest of borders. Sages give off a musky aroma, particularly in the heat of the sun. The best for cooking is the common garden sage, *S. officinalis*, which has bright blue flowers and can be sown indoors in spring. The white-flowering version is 'Albiflora'. 'Purpurascens' is one of the finest of purple-leaf plants and looks beautiful with grays and silvers, as well as with greens and purples. 'Icterina' and 'Tricolor' (less hardy) are excellent variegated forms that can be bought as container-grown plants. Plant sage in well-drained soil in a sunny spot or in a container. The plants need to be renewed every four or five years by layering or taking cuttings.

OPPOSITE, LEFT **When grown in rich, well-drained soil, curly parsley produces cascades of emerald green.**

OPPOSITE, CENTER AND RIGHT **Rosemary is a herb that has it all. It is an evergreen with startling flowers, aromatic foliage, and forms that range from upright through to ground cover, and even include trailing varieties.**

RIGHT **New growth of** Salvia officinalis **'Purpurascens' is like velvet fountains. The vibrant new foliage makes an appealing contrast with the wisdom of the old.**

FAR RIGHT AND BELOW RIGHT **Variegated sage 'Icterina' is a fine ornamental, and the slightly more tender 'Tricolor' has margins tinged with pink. Both have a milder flavor than the green form. Sages need well-drained soil.**

BELOW, FAR RIGHT **Flowering sage adds a spectacular blue splash to a border, mixing beautifully with other plants.**

BELOW **Removing the flowers of buckler-leaf sorrel improves leaf production, but I like to leave it in flower.**

Satureja spp. **Savory**. Winter savory, *S. montana*, is an evergreen shrubby perennial with a neat growing habit that can reach a height of 1ft (30cm). It has pointed leaves and small white, pink, or purple flowers; the leaves can be harvested throughout the year. Summer savory (*S. hortensis*) is a good companion to beans, both in the garden and in the kitchen. Since the seed is fine and germination is erratic, sow savory under cover and transplant after all danger of frost has passed. Plant in well-drained soil in sun.

Symphytum officinale. **Comfrey**. Perennial. Comfrey is very beautiful when it begins to flower, with striking bell-shaped flowers that range from blue to white in spring and early summer. The lance-shaped leaves are slightly furry and appear to be full of vitality and health. The main problem with comfrey is its vigorous growing habit. The herb can be a bit of a bully in a small garden, and tends to colonize the bed. Plant comfrey in any soil in part shade or sun. To make a superb organic fertilizer—which is particularly good for tomatoes—steep comfrey leaves in a bucket of water over a week or two. Keep the bucket covered because comfrey smells unutterably foul while it is in the process of rotting.

Thymus. **Thyme**. Perennial. Thyme forms charming mounds covered in delicate flowers. They are lovely carpeters and edgers in the sun and are excellent for pots, cracks in paving, or dry sunny spots anywhere, releasing an invigorating scent when touched or walked upon—although I would recommend planting thymes in places where there is not too much foot traffic. The best for cooking is the garden thyme, *T. vulgaris*, upright and growing to 12in (30cm) with mauve flowers. 'Silver Posie' is a good silver-leaf variety. *T. serpyllum* is prostrate, and there are many varieties, including *T. coccineus* with magenta flowers. Lemon-scented varieties are particularly good in chicken and rice dishes. Thyme must be planted in well-drained soil because it hates damp soil in winter (as—much to my annoyance—I have discovered time and time again). Trim plants after flowering to encourage new growth.

RIGHT **Comfrey has earned a reputation as a colonizer and a bully, but comfrey growing in a compost heap brings a bit of poetry to a garden.**

BELOW **It is easy to fall in love with comfrey flowers, and the leaves are edible, though I would strongly recommend that the plants are grown to make organic fertilizer.**

THIS PAGE **Flowering thyme makes a scented aromatic carpet in a sunny border. The individual flowers—in pink, purple, or white—are beautifully delicate, and the massed effect is one of the finest sights in the garden. Thyme can also be effective in containers with adequate drainage. Vigorous varieties need to be cut back hard after flowering to retain their compactness.**

Growing vegetables can conjure up images of an allotment, an old cloth cap, a garden shed, and an aching back. Although all of these can still play a part in kitchen gardening, the emphasis has shifted to creativity and pleasure. Some vegetables, such as

vegetables

zucchini and runner beans, are seen to be among the finest ornamentals available to the gardener. And, although your onions and carrots may not win any prizes, stepping outside to pull a few fresh carrots, pluck a sweet and juicy tomato, or gather a few salad greens is a thrill not to be missed.

ABOVE LEFT **A garlic that hasn't been harvested produces a beautiful flower. I deliberately grow more garlic than I need for the kitchen and leave some in for the flowering.**

ABOVE RIGHT **An artichoke is a superb ornamental that can look imposing and glorious in a garden.**

vegetable basics

Browsing through a seed catalog on a winter's evening is likely to send your taste buds and your imagination into overdrive. From the comfort of an easy chair, it takes great self-control and careful planning not to order an excessive number of seeds—and, even then, you are likely to be storing leftover seeds for at least a year. Be realistic about the space and commitment you want to give to growing vegetables, and if you are new to kitchen gardening, start with one of the easier crops.

Sowing seeds Most annual vegetables can be grown from seed. For an early start indoors, use the house or greenhouse when the weather is too cold or unreliable outside. Follow the instructions on the back of the seed packet to determine sowing dates. As with herbs, the basic equipment is a pot or small propagator and ready-made seed-starting soil. Use a container with good drainage and sow into moist soil, leaving a couple of hours between watering and sowing to allow excess water to drain off

PLANTING SEEDS
Some seeds, such as these beans, can be planted directly into the garden after the frosts have gone. A late-planted bean can often catch up with pot-grown transplants, and will crop until late in the season.

PREPARING THE SOIL
A rake is one of those old-fashioned gardening implements that is an evocative reminder of times past, as well as being invaluable in creating a fine texture for the seedbed.

and to avoid 'damping off', a fungal disease that can kill the seedlings. A seed packet tends to contain enough seeds to satisfy an army, so use only a few, refold the packet, and seal with tape.

Seedlings jostling for space in a crowded container compete for light and moisture and are vulnerable to disease. When the plants are large enough to handle, prick them out and space them into a seed tray, modules, or pots, by using a plant label to dig them up and gently picking them up by a leaf.

Planting out Plant out tender varieties when all danger of frost has passed and the plants are big enough to handle. Harden them off by acclimatizing them to the cold, and make sure the soil is well prepared with plenty of garden soil. The main threat to these seedlings comes from slugs and snails, which adore fresh green growth.

Hardier early crops can be sown indoors in late winter and planted outside under cloches or cold frames, which help to keep the soil warm and protect the seedlings from frost. This accelerates growth and increases productivity, making possible a succession of crops. Less hardy plants can be planted out from mid spring without cover as long as they are hardened off.

Buying young plants from a reputable source is an excellent way to grow a few vegetables in a small garden. Planting a couple of zucchini, some tomatoes and beans, a box of broad beans, and rows of lettuce may not save you from having to visit the

NURTURING YOUNG PLANTS
Plastic bottles that have been cut off at the base make effective miniature cloches for individual plants early in the season. They offer good protection against cold, slugs, and snails.

RAISING SEEDLINGS

BELOW AND BOTTOM LEFT AND RIGHT **All sorts of containers can be used for raising seedlings. Polystyrene cups are a good choice because the polystyrene acts as an excellent insulator against the cold and heat. Don't forget to poke a couple of drainage holes in the bottom of each cup before adding soil. Traditional plastic pots can be reused, though it is worth cleaning them well between plantings to prevent diseases.**

PROTECTIVE MEASURES

ABOVE **Corn seedlings take their first trip out of the greenhouse to harden off. Seedlings raised inside will be accustomed to relatively warm conditions and tend to be slightly tender when first put outside, so put them in an area with some protection and take them in if the nights are cold.**

BELOW **When planting out a young plant, don't worry if it looks a bit floppy for a couple of days—it will soon recover. Water copiously and watch out for slugs and snails, which seem to like young succulent leaves. I use a bit of vermiculite around the base of particularly vulnerable seedlings.**

SUPPORT FOR CLIMBERS

LEFT **Putting together a structure to support climbing vegetables such as runner beans is one of the most enjoyable jobs of the growing season. I use bamboo canes, and tie them at the top with string or plastic-coated wire. Push the canes into the ground until they are firm and tie in tightly and neatly at the top. The structure needs to be fairly strong, since it will have to hold quite a weight of mature plants, and must be resistant to wind.**

LEFT **A tidy-looking structure is more attractive to look at, especially because a lopsided pyramid can be disorientating and is more likely to collapse when covered in foliage. The newly planted vegetables may take a little while to get started, but it is amazing how quickly the frame becomes a wall of green—so take care to place it where the green curtain will not obscure too much of the garden.**

supermarket, but they are a welcome addition to the garden and the plate. Growing edibles on a small scale also gives you plenty of opportunities to experiment—especially valuable in your first years as a kitchen gardener.

Plants are available from garden centers and by mail order and are supplied in several different forms. Plants grown in pots and six-packs are available early in the season. Care should be taken when removing them and separating them because the roots are often entwined, and they need gently teasing to pull them apart.

Plugs—which are grown in a box divided into individual cells—are less vulnerable to root disturbance when planting out, although they are sometimes too small to plant out immediately. You can buy larger individual plants that are ready to plant out. Tomatoes come in a huge

range of varieties and pot sizes, from a 3in (8cm) baby to a mature tumbling hanging basket. All the same warnings apply as for herbs—particularly to take care early in the season with vegetables grown under cover, since the soft new growth of most vegetables is even more vulnerable than herbs to cold weather. Slugs and snails can devour this soft new growth in the blink of an eye—you can help to protect it by cutting a plastic bottle in half and using it as a mini cloche.

Structural plantings Climbing and scrambling vegetables are total charmers, and are among the loveliest of plants for a mixed garden. Beans have a flexibility and versatility that allows you to paint pictures by leading them into spaces along a cane or up a string. The framework on which beans climb can vary from existing walls to trellis, chainlink fence or tripods—or you can be really creative by training them up fanned-out

HARVESTING

LEFT AND FAR LEFT **Gathering the first onions of the season is a satisfying moment for the kitchen gardener. Nature signals that they are ready to harvest when the tops gracefully bow down and the leaves begin to dry out.**

BELOW LEFT TO RIGHT **The feel, taste, and smell of freshly harvested potatoes or carrots capture one of the essences of kitchen garden pleasures. Carrots can be pulled out by the foliage from a light soil, but in a heavier soil it is worth loosening them with a fork to ease them free.**

canes or along string suspended from overhead wires. This sort of artistry adds a new vertical dimension to a garden and, like a living sculpture, changes over time.

Among other vegetables that make excellent vertical highlights are squashes and gourds, cucumber, and peas. More vigorous varieties of gourds can get quite heavy and are likely to need more substantial canes.

Feeding Provided that the soil is healthy and appropriate for the crop, little regular feeding is required for crops in the ground. Adding compost and manure will provide them with most of their vital nutrients. The three main nutrients needed are nitrogen (N) for leaf growth, phosphorus (P) for root growth, and potassium (K) for flowering and fruiting. Look for fertilizers that have been formulated to promote the type of crop you

FAR LEFT **Beets should be lifted with a gentle tug and a twist—the leaves are also edible.**

LEFT **A lettuce as large and splendid as this 'Verde d'Inverno' calls for a leisurely alfresco meal with friends.**

BELOW LEFT AND RIGHT **A newly harvested parsnip is a reminder of the hidden world beneath the soil. Garlic pulled in late summer can be stored for ages in a cool dry place.**

want: high nitrogen for leafy crops, high phosphates for roots, and high potassium for fruiting crops. Plants in containers will need more regular feeding—and the same rule applies.

Rotation Because vegetables have specific soil and mineral requirements, they should be grown in different places in the garden from year to year – a technique called rotation. This is particularly important in the case of brassicas, which are vulnerable to club root, an extremely debilitating fungal disease that can easily build up in the soil.

Pests and diseases There are many pests and diseases that affect vegetables, although many of these are kept at a manageable level in the mixed garden. The more intensive your planting becomes, the more work and knowledge is required to prevent a small and harmless infection becoming a more difficult problem.

root vegetables

Root vegetables are a magical addition to the garden—partly because of the mystery of the crop that lies underneath the soil. The childlike expectation associated with pulling carrots, seeing the shape and size of a new parsnip, or digging up and counting a crop of succulent new potatoes introduces a new dimension to growing edibles.

Root vegetables prefer well-drained soil with few stones that has been enriched the previous year with manure—apart from potatoes, which appreciate manure at any time. Most prefer sun. They resent being moved and are best sown in position unless they have been started in biodegradable containers.

Beta vulgaris. **Beet**. Beets have bold leaves and come not only in red but also in yellow or white, and even with striped flesh. 'Bull's Blood' is the most vibrant, with burgundy foliage that looks great when planted in a group, contrasting with other leaf shades. The globe types grow well in pots. Sow bolt-resistant varieties outdoors from early spring. Young leaves are lovely in salads; older ones can be cooked as greens.

Brassica napus Napobrassica Group. **Rutabaga**. Rutabaga is not very ornamental. It prefers cool, damp conditions. Sow disease-resistant seed outside in early summer and harvest from fall onwards. Keep well watered to aid growth and to help control flea beetle.

Brassica rapa Rapifera Group. **Turnip**. Turnip grows fast—some mature in about 60 days—and comes in designer ranges, but is not very ornamental. Turnip can take a little shade and likes cool damp conditions. Grow as rutabaga. Harvest entire crop in fall before they go woody, and store.

Daucus carota. **Carrot**. With its attractive feathery leaves, carrot looks good as spot planting in gaps or in clumps, particularly near other fine

OPPOSITE, LEFT AND RIGHT **Beets are attractive foliage plants that look especially effective in a group. I like the red etching that seems to flow from the base.**

LEFT AND FAR LEFT **The whispering leaves of carrot help to lighten an area, and the short-rooted varieties are easy to grow in containers.**

BELOW **Parsnip is one of those vegetables in which the prize below the soil is more interesting than the architecture above.**

foliage such as achillea and nigella. The miniature and short-rooted varieties are good in containers. Sow early types in spring followed by a main crop in early summer. Growing in a mixed garden helps to reduce risk of attack by carrot fly. Planting near onions also helps. If it is left to grow for a second year, carrot produces attractive flowers, which appeal to beneficial insects.

Helianthus tuberosus. **Jerusalem artichoke**. Perennial. Jerusalem artichoke grows up to 10ft (3m) tall with sage-green leaves. It makes a useful screening plant, providing shelter from the wind and blocking out undesirable views. Can be used as a living frame for annual climbers such as sweet peas or the lovely yellow-flowered canary creeper. Slightly more compact varieties are available. 'Fuseau' is particularly good for cooking. The flowers resemble small sunflowers in late summer. Plant tubers about 6in (15cm) deep in mid spring. Stake taller varieties if in a windy spot, and start to harvest in fall when leaves turn brown.

Pastinaca sativa. **Parsnip**. Parsnip is not particularly ornamental unless left for a second year, when it produces an enormous head of seeds and flowers, which attract insects. Sow seed in late spring, three seeds to a planting hole, and thin out weaker seedlings. In a mixed, border grow shorter-rooted varieties, which can be harvested without too much disturbance.

Raphanus sativus. **Radish**. Radish is quick to grow but not as easy as people think. The plants themselves are not especially attractive, although letting some go to seed is worthwhile. Sow in any soil from spring to early fall in sun or dappled shade. Podding radishes such as 'Munchen Bier' combine beautiful flowers with unusual edible pods.

Solanum tuberosum. **Potato**. Try a few 'earlies', which will thrive in a barrel or in a small space in the garden—the foliage is a restful green and the taste bears no comparison to supermarket potatoes. The early potatoes grow fast and are less prone than the maincrops to pests and diseases. Start potatoes into growth in early spring by laying tubers in a shallow tray in light dry conditions, with the eyes uppermost. Plant when the sprouts are about 1in (2cm) long. Potato is a heavy feeder, so add plenty of rich organic matter and manure to the soil. Plant about 6in (15cm) deep and 1ft (30cm) apart. As the shoots grow, keep earthing them up to encourage more tubers and prevent greening. Potato is ready to harvest when in flower. Varieties such as 'Swift' and 'Rocket' are fun to grow in large containers.

ABOVE **Radishes take only a short time to mature and have a reputation for being one of the easiest vegetables to grow, but they can disappoint.**

LEFT **Although the potato may be an uninspiring plant in isolation, there is something wholesome and earthy about having potatoes in your garden, where they add the sense of satisfaction associated with being a provider.**

ABOVE **The magic of the harvest is never better captured than in the discovery of a potato crop under the soil. You may sometimes find a good crop spreading out a surprising distance from the plant.**

bulb and stem vegetables

A few asparagus spears freshly cut from the back garden can fill you with gardening pride. A small group of onions and shallots conveys a vivid sense of spring's potential with their fresh green growth, and of summer's abundant harvest when the leaves begin to wilt. Even in a small pot, onions and shallots are an atmospheric and worthy addition to a garden. A string of harvested home-grown garlic is a reminder of the season's wealth.

Allium cepa and *Allium cepa* Aggregatum Group. **Onion** and **shallot**. Onion and shallots look great in a garden, and both can thrive in containers. Shallots produce masses of fresh foliage, which is a beautiful pale green, but this dies back rather messily before the vegetable is harvested. Buy sets that have been heat-treated against bolting and disease. They tolerate most soils as long as they can get some sun. Try to plant in a different place in the garden in consecutive years. Before planting, cut off the foliage to prevent birds pulling them out, and plant just below the surface. Main-crop onions and shallots should be planted in early spring, and Japanese onions in late summer. If you need to protect onions and shallots from squirrels, lay old canes over the newly planted bed, or start them in biodegradable pots and plant them out when rooted. When the leaves flop over, they are ready to harvest. Dig up carefully and leave to dry in the sun or inside until the skins are brown. Store in an airy place.

Allium fistulosum. **Welsh onion**. Hardy perennial; virtually evergreen. The small bulbs and leaves can be eaten. Sow in spring or early summer in soil similar to that for onions. I love the vibrant foliage and the bobbing flowers. Mature plants can be split and replanted in fall.

LEFT, FROM LEFT TO RIGHT
There are few sights more rewarding than a crop of onions ready for the cooking pot or storage box.
The flowers of the Welsh onion make a refreshingly cheerful sight in summer.
Shallots are one of my favorite garden crops. A single bulb becomes a clump within six months, and the cheerful spring flowers are especially appealing.

FAR LEFT **Architectural forms have traditionally abounded in the garden, and some edibles—such as this leek, with its dramatic shape and magnificent foliage—are well suited to becoming focal points.**

LEFT **Garlic is worth a place in most gardens. Apart from being easy to grow, it occupies little space, helps to ward off pests and is completely delicious when eaten fresh.**

BELOW LEFT **It is satisfying to leave a couple of garlic plants in the ground to flower, especially when they take up so little space and the results are so striking. The beguiling mild scent of garlic is a surprising bonus.**

RIGHT **Celeriac foliage has a strong celery flavor, but more substantial is the swollen bulb at the base of the stem, which is either cooked or grated and eaten raw in salads.**

Allium porrum. **Leek**. With its upright plume of green, gray-blue or even purple-tinged foliage, the leek brings an architectural accent to a garden. Given a sunny spot and fertile soil, it needs little attention. Sow indoors in spring. When transplanting, make a little vertical hole 6in (15cm) deep and drop the leek into it, dribbling in a little water before covering the roots with fine soil. If surplus leeks are left in for a second year rather than pulled, they produce attractive large white flowers tinged with pink.

Allium sativum. **Garlic**. Garlic is simple to grow and looks decorative in rows between crops or as a spot planting in small spaces. I like to have a few in pots on a window ledge. Buy bulbs specifically for planting. Divide up the cloves and plant them in fall, with the tips pointing up, about 1in (2.5cm) deep. Garlic likes an airy, sunny spot and prospers in any free-draining fertile soil. Early spring planting produces smaller bulbs. Harvest in late summer when the leaves droop. Leave to dry in the sun or a shed. Plant garlic in a different area of the garden each year to avoid the build-up of pests and diseases. Fresh young shoots are delicious in salads, but don't pick too many because this will reduce the size of the bulb.

Apium graveolens var. *dulce*. **Celery**. Leaf celery for soups is simpler to grow that stem celery; its bushy, clean-cut foliage is quite attractive and looks at home in an ornamental border. But self-blanching varieties have made growing stem celery less work since they do not require earthing up (which involves covering the stem with soil). Sow in early spring under cover on the surface of the soil because the seeds need light. Plant out in early summer in sun or partial shade in rich fertile moist soil. Keep well fed and watered.

Apium graveolens var. *rapaceum*. **Celeriac**. Celeriac is a slow-growing vegetable with a leaf like celery. Sow under cover in spring, and plant out well after frosts in sun or part shade in most soils. Keep well watered. Remove lower leaves from midsummer. Harvest from fall onwards.

Asparagus officinalis. **Asparagus**. Perennial. Asparagus has ferny foliage that looks beautiful in the background of a border or even as a summer hedge. I love the appearance of the new spears as they break the ground in spring. Asparagus plants consume quite a lot of space in relation to the amount harvested, but a single plant can be a beautiful addition to a garden. Asparagus can produce for twenty years, so it is worth preparing the soil well. Buy established 'crowns' and plant them in a sunny spot. Add plenty of organic matter and manure to the soil, and make sure that there is good drainage. Dig a trench 10in (25cm) deep and 1ft (30cm) wide. Make a ridge down the middle, lay the crowns on it 12–16in (30–40cm) apart, and backfill. Keep well watered. Asparagus should not be harvested until the second year, and then only sparingly. After that, it can be picked for about six weeks before being left to recoup. Cut off the foliage when yellow in fall and mulch well. Asparagus can be grown in very large containers.

Foeniculum vulgare var. *dulce*. **Florence fennel**. Florence fennel, with its feathery leaves, is as elegant as it is delicious, but it can bolt (go to seed) if allowed to dry out. It is attractive against bare soil or amid low green foliage. It is best sown outside when the weather is warm. Choose bolt-resistant seed and scatter it thinly in well-drained soil in a sunny place. Make sure that it never dries out.

ABOVE **When asparagus emerges from the ground, it looks wonderfully enticing. A good crop may not be ready to harvest for three years, but it is worth the wait.**

LEFT **Florence fennel is a bright spark when grown well, although it can be a little temperamental.**

fruiting vegetables

Fruiting vegetables are among the most ornamental and spectacular of the edibles.
A garden of any size would benefit from a couple of tomato plants covered in ripening
fruit, chile peppers dripping in spicy jewels, a small plot of corn blessed by the sun,
and in a larger space, artichokes glorious and imposing in bud and flower.

Fruiting vegetables, particularly the lower-growing varieties, need protection from slugs
and snails. Most prefer a sheltered sunny location and well-drained soil. Feed with tomato
or comfrey fertilizer to encourage flowering and fruiting.

Capsicum annuum Grossum Group. **Sweet pepper**. A tender crop that requires as much
sun as possible, sweet pepper can struggle to survive during a cool summer. It comes in
many shapes and colors, including black. Peppers are very successful in pots, which can
be moved into positions where they get the most sun. They tend to attract aphids—try to
control these before they swamp the plants. Sow seed in late spring or buy small plants
and plant out when warm in pots or a border.

Capsicum annuum Longum Group. (or Capiscum spp.) **Chile pepper**. Chiles makes a wonderfully decorative container plant with its neat foliage, masses of star-shaped flowers, and an abundance of elegant fruits, which come in orange and purple as well as red. I find chiles easier than sweet peppers, and much more prolific. They can look a bit grumpy on cool evenings, when the leaves sulk, but don't worry—they recover the next day. Buy plants or sow seed indoors in late spring and wait until early summer to put them out.

Cynara cardunculus. **Cardoon**. Perennial. A dramatic relative of globe artichoke, cardoon—with its gray-blue foliage and thistle flowers—is worth growing in a large border for its looks alone. It becomes an architectural centerpiece of the border. Blanch the edible stems by bunching them together and wrapping them about three weeks before harvesting in fall. Cardoon tolerates some frost and requires good drainage.

OPPOSITE **In a warm protected garden, a sweet pepper makes a beautiful ornamental, especially in late summer. I like to leave the fruit on as long as possible because a well-grown sweet pepper is a truly spectacular sight.**

THIS PAGE **There is a tremendous range of chiles available to the gardener. I grow them for the lovely fruit alone, since they are slightly too hot for my taste. The black-fruited beauty 'Filius Blue' (right) is one of the finest looking.**

Cynara scolymus. **Globe artichoke**. Perennial in mild-winter areas. Globe artichoke is grown not only for its gourmet flower buds but also as a stately ornamental. It has gray serrated leaves and huge buds (the artichokes), which, if allowed to flower, open to enormous blue thistle-like flowers. Artichokes tolerate some frost and require a sunny spot in well-drained soil with plenty of organic matter to stop them from drying out in summer. They grow into a big clump, so need plenty of space and tend to become the star of the show. Mulch and keep well watered, particularly in the first season. Good cropping starts in the second year.

Lycopersicon esculentum. **Tomato**. The tomato is astonishing for the sheer diversity of its shape, form, and size—ranging from the giant beefsteak tomato down to miniatures that are suitable for growing in containers on a windowsill or even in hanging baskets. The compact varieties make very successful fillers in a garden as an alternative to bedding plants. Outdoor varieties have made tomato growing much simpler. These prefer a sheltered location. The bush types are the easiest to look after and need no staking. The upright ones need support in the form of canes, surrounding plants or a wall. Pinch out side shoots and the growing tip when it reaches the required height. Either grow from seed under cover or buy small plants. Transplant in early summer into a soil rich in organic matter in full sun. Keep constantly watered but not too wet—and try to keep the water off the foliage.

THIS PAGE **Artichoke is a tough perennial once established—as well as being one of the most statuesque and beautiful of the edibles. Although artichokes need plenty of space, I use mine to create a focal point and add substance to a small border. Some of the continental varieties are even more beautiful.**

OPPOSITE **Tomatoes must be one of the most diverse groups of edibles, with a vast range of habits and fruit. Many of the best varieties are available by mail order. I particularly like the incredibly long trusses of 'Broad Ripple Yellow Currant'. The flowers are insignificant on their own, but have a discreet charm in the right setting.**

RIGHT **Eggplant comes in many shapes and sizes. This 'Louisiana Long Green' grew in a conservatory.**

FAR RIGHT **The sumptuous color of traditional eggplant wins it a place in a warm garden on looks alone.**

BELOW RIGHT AND FAR RIGHT, ABOVE AND BELOW **Fresh corn should ideally be eaten the moment after it has left the plant. The red-leaved corn produces one of the most graceful of foliage displays.**

Solanum melongena. **Eggplant**. Eggplant is an attractive plant with soft velvety foliage, lavender-blue flowers, and sumptuous fruit. It adds a really exotic feeling to a hot garden, and is particularly beautiful with grays, blues, and purples. Grow eggplant in a greenhouse in cooler climates or under a cloche. Sow seed in very early spring indoors and keep them warm. Plant outside in late spring after any danger of frosts has passed in a hot sheltered spot or in a container.

Zea mays. **Corn**. Resembling a huge grass, corn is a taste sensation when freshly picked. It makes a great bold statement in the garden, but you don't get many cobs for your space. Sow seed from mid spring onwards inside or a few weeks later outside, or plant out bought plants in a sunny position as soon as the soil is warm. A group of at least five is best since corn is wind-pollinated. The soil should be free draining but with plenty of organic matter incorporated. The cobs are ripe when the tassles turn brown. Try the Early Xtra Sweet varieties.

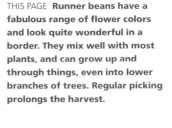

THIS PAGE **Runner beans have a fabulous range of flower colors and look quite wonderful in a border. They mix well with most plants, and can grow up and through things, even into lower branches of trees. Regular picking prolongs the harvest.**

podding vegetables

Runner beans twining up a fence or into a tree satisfy a basic yearning for beauty and nourishment. Freshly picked broad beans have a succulence that can't be bought at a supermarket, and peas straight off the plant are a sweet and magical morsel. Peas and beans are nitrogen fixers and, dug into the soil after harvest, act as a green manure, boosting fertility. Podding vegetables favor moisture-retentive soil with plenty of organic matter added (but not freshly manured) and, when young, need protection from slugs and snails.

Phaseolus coccineus. **Runner bean**. Runner bean is beautiful in leaf and flower as well as providing a prodigious harvest. It combines well with most garden plants, but looks especially beautiful when teamed with sweet peas. There are dwarf varieties that can be grown in containers, and the tall climbers make statuesque ornamentals in the garden, grown over poles, teepees, trellises or more creative sculptural structures. Plant under cover or outside in mid spring in a warm sheltered spot. The roots should never be allowed to dry out, so before planting prepare a deep bed enriched with homemade compost. Climbing varieties can put up with some shade as long as they can get to the sun.

Phaseolus vulgaris. **Snap bean (french bean)**. The snap bean is prolific and comes with flat or rounded 'pencil' pods in purple and gold—among other colors. There are dwarf varieties available that grow well in pots and near the edges of beds; climbers that combine beauty in leaf, flower and form and are very productive for the space they take up. Sow inside in spring or outside when the soil is warm. Prepare soil as for runner beans. Late sowings up until midsummer can give a good harvest into fall. Plant close together in a sheltered sunny place. Water when dry.

Pisum sativum. **Pea** and **sugar peas**. The pea plant can look very appealing when supported in an attractive way, but if the support structure is a mess, it tends to look untidy. Early peas are more compact growers and tend to pod less. Petit pois are smaller peas with a good flavor; the wrinked-seeded varieties tend to be less hardy than the smooth-seeded ones. There are also 'semi-leafless' varieties which need little support, dwarfs for containers, and sugar peas, or edible-pod peas. Sow outside from mid spring. Too rich a soil will produce more leaves than peas. Peas like a cool, sheltered location and can take a little shade. Don't let them dry out.

ABOVE LEFT **Its purple pods makes the french bean 'Purple Teepee' a stylish addition to a garden. It will thrive in a large container if well-watered in summer.**

ABOVE **An emerging bean is a fascinating and reassuring sight in the garden.**

OPPOSITE, ABOVE **Edible-pod peas scrambling up a frame add delicacy to a border.**

OPPOSITE, BELOW **Broad beans mature early in the season and are very hardy. The crimson-flowered variety is particularly lovely.**

Vicia faba. **Broad bean**. Broad beans don't look much at first sight, but they have attractive flowers, a sweet scent and a delicious taste. Dwarf varieties are best for the mixed garden and look good in large containers. If picked young, the entire pod can be cooked. An early crop can be sown outside in fall helping to reduce the damage done by blackfly, followed by a maincrop in early spring. They prefer the sun though can tolerate partial shade. Water well between flowering and harvest.

Miscellaneous *Lablab purpureus* The lablab bean is one of the most beautiful climbing plants, with purple and pink flowers followed by deep purple beans. Sunlight through the beans looks almost magical. Cultivate like snap beans, but needs a higher temperature. Plant in full sun.

brassicas and spinach

Brassicas and spinach are fine foliage plants with colors ranging from emerald green to purple, red, and ruby. Wonderful chards deserve pride of place in a border, mixing confidently with ornamentals, and Italian black cabbage is sumptuous and elegant.

To discourage cabbage root fly on brassicas, cut a piece of carpet pad into a 6in (15cm) square and use it as a collar by slitting it in the center and creating a hole large enough for the plant to fit through the middle. Brassicas should be planted quite deeply when transplanting. There are quite a few pests and diseases that can affect brassicas—so avoid planting them in the same spot each year.

Atriplex hortensis. **Red orache**. Red orache, or red mountain spinach, with its beet-red translucent leaves, grows fast up to 4ft (1.2m) high and makes a fine ornamental. Looks lovely as a warm splash mixed into a border. The young leaves add color to salads, and the older leaves can be cooked. Sow outside from spring to summer in full sun or partial shade. It will self-seed freely once established. Interesting variants are the Plume Series with yellow, green, or burgundy flowers and foliage.

Beta vulgaris Cicla Group. **Chard**. Chard is one of the most valuable ornamental vegetables. It makes a big colorful splash—particularly the ruby varieties—in the garden or in containers. It can be planted singly or in groups in a bed. Both flowers and foliage offer lovely contrasts. With the sun behind them, the leaves of chard are almost luminous. Sow indoors in spring for a summer and fall crop, and sow in sun or light shade in late summer or early fall outside to overwinter (in mild-winter areas) for an early crop the following year. Regular harvesting of the outer leaves encourages succulent young growth. You can keep the fresh leaves coming during winter with cloche protection—though in a mild winter my chard kept on growing when put near a wall. Leaf beet, or perpetual spinach, belongs to this group and is a good alternative to spinach, being hardier and easier to grow.

Brassica oleracea Acephala Group. **Kale**. Kale has some real stars in the family. The Italian black cabbage (cavalo nero) 'Nero di Toscana' is simply beautiful in the

garden with its creased bluish gray foliage that fits nicely into many parts of the border. There are few plants that have such a lovely leaf and grow with such refined enthusiasm. They look particularly fine with other foliage plants and sparked up by some reds and blues. In mild-winter areas, late-sown Italian black cabbage can be harvested throughout winter. Sow in early spring in the ground for summer crops, and later for fall and winter crops. Plant firmly and stake taller types. Kales are hardy and easy to grow. They yield through to spring and taste their best after a frost.

Brassica oleracea Botrytis Group. **Cauliflower**. Cauliflower is difficult to grow successfully and has a low yield for the space it takes up. Late summer and fall types grow faster and are the safest bet. They need some sun and shelter plus very regular watering. Sow in mid spring.

OPPOSITE, ABOVE **Orache is one of those gems that is less well known than it should be. The leaf color and texture are superb, making it worthy of a place in the border.**

OPPOSITE, BELOW LEFT AND RIGHT **Over-wintered ruby chard has the most intense color; it is both easy to grow and good to eat.**

ABOVE LEFT AND CENTER **Italian black cabbage in the frost brings atmosphere to a garden and greens to the plate. It is one of the finest foliage plants in the garden at any time of year.**

ABOVE RIGHT **Although I find the taste of the curly kale a little off-putting, the foliage is a fascinating addition to the border.**

RIGHT **Unfortunately, cauliflower can be a bit temperamental—so a well-grown specimen is a prize to be treasured.**

Brassica oleracea Capitata Group. **Cabbage**. Cabbage can be grown all year, and there is a wide choice of beautiful form and foliage, including red cabbage, which looks lovely with the deep blue of lobelia or the purple of *Verbena bonariensis*. Sow bolt-resistant seed inside or out according to season. Cabbage likes cool conditions and can take a little shade. Cabbage loopers, a type of caterpillar, can be a problem; either pick them off by hand or use biological control.

Brassica oleracea Gemmifera Group. **Brussels sprouts**. A slow-growing hardy stalwart, brussels sprouts look a bit clumsy, but the red-leaved form is fine-looking. Sow early cultivars under cover and transplant in early summer, followed by mid or late-season types. Sprouts like a sheltered, reasonably sunny spot. They need staking. Flavor improves after a frost.

Brassica oleracea Italica Group. **Sprouting broccoli**. Sprouting broccoli flowers for three months from early in the year and is delicious cut fresh from the garden. The handsome plants thrive in a mixed border. Sow thinly in mid spring for an early crop, or in summer for a later one. The soil should be free draining, but not so rich as to encourage leaf over shoot growth. Broccoli likes a sunny spot out of the wind. 'Calabrese', which has a beautiful green head, is difficult to grow.

Spinacia oleracea. **Spinach**. Spinach is a temperamental crop that bolts in hot weather. But, given good rich soil, copious water and dappled shade, the pale new leaves make a gentle and lovely ground cover. Summer varieties can be sown every few weeks for a constant supply. New Zealand spinach (*Tetragonia tetragonioides*) withstands hot weather without bolting.

74

TOP ROW, LEFT TO RIGHT **Cabbage grown in a garden can be both attractive and rewarding. I like these 'Minicole' cabbages planted with annual ornamental grasses. Red cabbage (also bottom row, left), one of the loveliest of foliage plants, would add grace to any border. Cabbage is a quintessential kitchen garden plant that helps to create the sense of a fertile environment. Purple sprouting broccoli can be picked very early in the year. 'Calabrese' broccoli has a weird and wonderful head, but it can be hard to grow successfully, particularly if the weather is hot and dry.**

BOTTOM ROW, CENTER AND RIGHT **Though slightly tender, New Zealand spinach (center) is easier to grow in dry warm conditions than ordinary spinach—which positively glows with health on a drizzly day.**

75

cucumber and squash

Cucumber and squash—also known as cucurbits—can make rewarding residents in a garden, for their sculptural as well as their culinary attributes. Squash climbing up a tripod while the fruit obstinately dangles down, and zucchini blowing out huge yellow flowers, are followed by small balloons of green or large variegated zeppelins. Their enormous leaves put many ornamentals in the shade.

Cucurbits need to be protected from slugs and snails, particularly when they are young. Before planting, dig in plenty of organic matter and well-rotted manure. They all need plenty of moisture, so don't let them dry out—those that do are prone to mildew.

Cucumis sativus. **Cucumber**. Outdoor cucumber tends to be rough-skinned and spiney. The bush types can be cultivated in large containers, and the climbers look decorative grown on teepees. Look for modern varieties that are self-fertile and more resistant to cold and disease. Cucumber is no longer simply long and green in appearance; there are also white, yellow and even round forms. Cucumber can look rather messy, particularly near the end of season. It is very sensitive to wind. Sow inside in mid spring or outside in late spring. Plant in sun or partial shade.

Cucurbita pepo. **Zucchini** and other green summer squashes. Zucchini has handsome broad leaves and huge yellow trumpet flowers followed by a large quantity of fruit, which can be green, yellow or striped, cylindrical or round. The most ornamental types have a silver gray marking on the leaves. They grow large and tend to bully plants close to them, so give them plenty of space. Zucchini is great planted near the edge of a raised bed to tumble over the side. It can cope with partial shade but does best in full sun. Plant seed inside in early spring or in the garden when the danger of frost has passed. Can look magnificent in large

containers, particularly when in bloom. The flowers are delicious to eat—pick the male ones, which will not set fruit. Summer squash tend to flower and therefore fruit less.

Cucurbita maxima and *Cucurbita moschata*. **Pumpkin** and **squash.** Pumpkin is the true giant of the gourd family, needing four months of sunshine to mature; it is generally grown only for Halloween or, where there is plenty of space, for showing. Squash, which comes in myriad forms (both warty and smooth), is both fun to grow and good to eat. It adds real joy to a garden when grown over a pergola or teepee, and looks wonderful in an herbaceous border. The summer varieties, which include the scalloped pattypan, ball and crookneck types, should be eaten when picked, whereas the winter ones store well. Grow in the same way as zucchini.

OPPOSITE, BELOW **Zucchini are rewarding and easy to grow, but they tend to occupy a lot of space. The blowsy flowers are a joyous and captivating sight in summer.**

OPPOSITE, ABOVE **Cucumbers have been a bit windblown in my garden, so I think it is worth finding a sheltered place to grow them in. Look for varieties that are more disease-resistant.**

THIS PAGE **Pumpkins and squashes are not just for Halloween; the foliage is luxuriant, and squash can be grown up tripods—or hung from overhead wires to create interesting focal points.**

ABOVE **One of my kitchen garden essentials, arugula often produces seed, which can germinate the following year. Even a few leaves of arugula will spice up a green salad.**

OPPOSITE, TOP ROW, LEFT **The unique red foliage of 'Merveille des Quatre Saisons' adds to the palette of edibles.**

OPPOSITE, TOP ROW, RIGHT **These young seedlings are ready to be transplanted into the garden, where they will start their short life before being tossed into the salad bowl.**

OPPOSITE, BOTTOM ROW, LEFT TO RIGHT **'Verde d'Inverno' has tempting blush-pink foliage.
If a lettuce is cut down, it will sometimes produce small leaves that can be picked later.
Cut-and-come-again red 'Salad Bowl' always finds its way into my border.**

salad greens

Salad greens fit very comfortably into today's gardens. They are quick to mature, delightful to look at, and can be grown in small spaces. When you have a container full of cut-and-come-again lettuce, the red hues of 'Lollo Rossa' bubbling around the edge of a raised bed, and the peppery cut-leaf arugula used to fill in between shrubs, it takes no more than a leisurely stroll around the garden to fill your salad bowl with delicate leaves. Salad greens need protection from slugs and snails, which adore them. If you are growing the vegetables in pots, rub petroleum jelly around the outer rim under the leaf line before planting.

Cichorium endiva. **Endive.** Curly endive is the most attractive endive for a garden.It looks particularly appealing as a frilly edging to a border or mixed in with other salad greens such as 'Lollo Rossa' and it can tolerate dappled shade. Sow in light, free-draining soil. Keep well watered.

Cichorium intybus. **Chicory.** For an easy life, choose the 'non-forcing types' of chicory (which include the popular radicchio). They can be grown decoratively in containers or in the garden and provide designer salad leaves as a pick-and-come-again crop. Sow from late spring in a sunny spot. Start picking the leaves about six weeks later. If you cut out the whole head of chicory but leave the root, it will sprout again. Leave a couple of chicory plants in the ground for their marvelous tall blue flowers from midsummer to mid fall.

Eruca vesicaria. **Arugula.** Expensive in the supermarket, this fashionable hot salad leaf is easy to grow and thrives in a container or even in a hanging basket. Makes a useful space-filler in a border. Sow seed every few weeks from mid spring to early midsummer in dappled shade or sun. In mild climates, sow in the fall for a winter crop. Pick off the flower buds regularly to prevent flowering and going to seed. The forms with more pronounced cut leaves tend to be a lot spicier, particularly if they have overwintered.

Lactuca sativa. **Lettuce.** The choice of lettuce includes head, loose-leaf and romaine (cos) types, but the best lettuces for most small gardens and containers are the cut-and-come-again varieties. Quick and easy to grow, they make a good edging to a raised bed and can be used for underplanting where there is dappled shade. All can be sown or planted a few weeks apart, providing non-stop lettuce throughout summer, even in a window box. Make sure that there is plenty of organic matter in the soil. They can tolerate some shade and make great space-fillers. Try black-seeded 'Simpson' with attractive pale leaves and 'Lollo Rossa' with reddish wavy leaves, though there are many more. If your lettuces flower, it is worth leaving them in the ground because some are simply marvelous.

There is something magical about picking and eating home-grown fruit. Fruits spend the summer maturing and ripening, promising so much and helping to reinforce the beauty of the seasons. The blossoms of spring and the

fruit

expectations of summer are followed by a fall harvest of unforgettable tastes and textures. For me, the memory of the freshly picked mulberries, apples, and plums of my childhood made it inevitable that I would, in time, enjoy the fruits of my own garden.

fruit basics

Once you have decided to grow fruit in your garden, you will find that the choice is mind-boggling. Few garden centers have a wide range of fruit—but the pictures and names of the plants that are on sale are so enticing that is hard to leave without a full cart and fantasies of self-sufficiency. The promise of bowls of freshly picked 'Autumn Britten' raspberries, trugs of russet apples, and a tree heavy with plums fill the mind with sepia images of a gentler era. In reality, your choice will be limited by the size of your garden. The starting point in a small garden is to find the appropriate variety grown on the appropriate rootstock.

Most fruit trees are grafted onto rootstocks that determine the speed of growth of the tree and its eventual size. Dwarfing rootstocks allow fruit to be grown in the smallest of spaces. They not only reduce the vigor of the trees but also encourage them to come into fruit earlier. Choose the rootstock to suit the space you have, but in poor soils use less dwarfing rootstocks because a tree planted in a poor soil has less vigor.

LEFT **Its blossom alone would be enough to recommend the apple as an ornamental tree.**

FAR LEFT **Ripe gooseberries are delicious picked straight from the bush, particularly if they are still warm from the sun. Nigella makes a fine partner for this bush.**

OPPOSITE, BELOW **Blackberry is one of the most satisfying crops in the garden. It does quite well in shade and rarely disappoints. *Verbena bonariensis* is an ornamental that grows beautifully with edibles.**

BELOW **A container-grown fruit bush that is rootbound needs to have its roots gently teased away from the root ball to help them to find water when planted in the ground.**

Pollination Fruit that is not self-fertile requires a pollinator to set fruit—otherwise you may be left with a lovely flowering tree that has a fine crop of leaves in fall. In areas with a wide diversity of trees, the likelihood is that one of them will be a pollinator, so in a densely gardened area it is often worth taking the risk of planting only one tree. In more isolated gardens, or if you want to be absolutely certain of having fruit, buy two trees that are compatible and that will flower at the same time to ensure good fruit set and harvest. Self-fertile trees ones that will set fruit without a pollinator—are ideal in the small garden, but the choice is more limited.

Buying fruit trees Fruit trees are usually sold as container-grown plants, which means that they can be bought and planted at any time of the year. But container-grown fruit trees tend to become potbound, and being in pots for a long time makes them vulnerable to pests and diseases. Ideally, you should find out when a local garden center has fresh stock and buy then. I think that fall and winter are the best time to buy because this gives the roots a chance to develop before the potentially dry summer period. The root system of a container-grown specimen tends to be unnaturally fibrous, so, when planting, always tease out the roots to encourage them to spread.

STAKING A FRUIT TREE

TOP ROW, LEFT TO RIGHT **One method of staking a small fruit tree is to hammer a stake in at an angle. Tie a tree tie around both the stake and the tree relatively low on the stem and secure well. Hammering a nail through the tie into the stake prevents slippage and bark damage.**

Buying berries and small fruits Although most berries and small fruits are available as ball-and-burlapped plants in the fall, they are often sold as containerized plants—which means that if you buy them before late spring they should be in good condition. Avoid ball-and-burlapped plants that look dried out—they have probably been left lying around for too long.

Bare-root plants are available only when the trees are dormant in fall and winter. Buy direct from a nursery or by mail order. They will have fewer roots than ball-and-burlapped plants—and it may look odd to have so much top and so little bottom. But the roots are much thicker and stronger and have developed more naturally, which will give the tree a better start.

Most fruit trees like protection from strong winds and early frosts. If your garden is in a frost pocket, choose late-flowering varieties. A fruit tree needs staking to give it just enough

RIGHT **When you have staked your fruit tree, water it well, then water well again. In a lawn, keep the grass 15in (40cm) away from the stem.**

SUMMER PRUNING

THIS PAGE **Summer prune an apple or pear (unless it is a variety that fruits on the tips of branches) by cutting the new lateral growth back to between three and five leaves of the old growth.**

ABOVE **It is important to use a sharp pruner because a ragged cut can crush the stem, causing damage where infection can enter.**

ABOVE RIGHT **Cut just above a bud so that there is no dieback.**

ABOVE FAR RIGHT **The new growth starts where there is a swelling in the stem. This helps to keep trained trees contained and encourages buds to form.**

help for the first couple of years, while allowing much of the stem to sway in the wind, which strengthens the tree. Once the roots have spread out, the stake is no longer needed. The mistake is to support the tree up the whole stem, which creates a long-term dependency with tragic withdrawals symptoms when the stake rots.

Planting Although a container-grown tree can be planted at any time of year, those planted in summer need a lot of watering. Dig a hole far bigger than the roots, and mix in plenty of garden compost, taking care to break up the bottom of the hole thoroughly. Sprinkle a couple of handfuls of bonemeal, and mix well in the hole, and water. When the tree is planted, it should end up at the same level as it was in the container. Backfill with the soil and compost mixture, then soak it, and soak again.

Bare-root trees must be planted in the dormant season, but never when the weather is freezing or the ground waterlogged. Bare-root trees are lifted and shipped immediately from a nursery, and the sooner they are back in the soil the better. Never let the roots dry out, and soak them in water while digging the hole. Plant at the level of the old soil mark; when filling in, move the tree up and down to get the soil to fill all the root spaces.

Feeding, watering and pruning Once planted, fruit trees are pretty easy to look after. They benefit from a couple of handfuls of bonemeal and fish emulsion in early spring, and some well-rotted manure is always a treat.

A mulch of hay or bark in spring will help to conserve moisture and suppress weeds. Watering, particularly when the fruit is swelling, is vital for a good crop. Water thoroughly so that the water soaks in and does not simply encourage surface roots, which are much more vulnerable to drying out.

The aim of pruning is to improve the health of a tree, to increase its flowering and fruiting potential, and to train the tree into a particular shape or to grow against a wall. Many new varieties, particularly those on dwarfing rootstocks, need little work and will fruit reasonably well if left undisturbed. Most fruit trees need an open structure, because air and sun helps to keep diseases away and ripen the fruit. Remove weak and diseased branches, dead branches and crossing branches that are congested. Prune in winter except

THIS PAGE **If an apple breaks off naturally from the tree when gently lifted, it has reached the perfect stage for picking and eating.**

OPPOSITE **Even a single fruit tree can conjure up the sense of being in an orchard, amid a mass planting. I love the informality of a carpet of grasses and wildflowers under a mature tree.**

for cherries and plums, which are susceptible to silver leaf disease and should be pruned during the growing season. Apples and pears can be lightly pruned in summer to help keep them manageable and put more energy into bud production for the following year.

Birds, pests and diseases While I encourage birds into the garden with bird houses and feeders, it is always disappointing when they find some of the growing fruit utterly irresistible.

Unfortunately, birds are often our main competitors for a good crop of fruit. Red currants, white currants, and cherries are particularly attractive to birds and—even though a mixed garden will help disguise the fruit trees—it is worth protecting them with bird netting, or, in a large enough garden, a separate fruit cage. Blackcurrants, raspberries, and strawberries are also vulnerable and would all benefit from being covered by some netting.

Many pests and diseases can attack fruit, though in a mixed garden they tend to be less destructive than in an orchard or mass planting. Some cause superficial damage to the fruit, which neither affects the flavor nor permanently damages the plant.

tree fruit

All the tree fruit included in this section is perennial, and once planted and established will continue to reward you for many years. A mature fruit tree in the garden is like an old friend—it should be treasured and cherished. Protect fruit from birds with bird netting.

Cydonia oblonga. **Quince**. Quince trees look old and twisted before their time. They have apple-blossom flowers and leathery leaves with furry underside that turn a buttercup shade in fall. Reaching around 7ft (more than 2m) at maturity, quince is the perfect tree to give a little antiquity to a new garden. Grows best in damp conditions and most soils, but is prone to mildew. Prune as necessary to get an open goblet shape. 'Smyrna' and 'Pineapple' are reliable, with large fruit.

Ficus carica. **Fig**. Fig is a handsome plant, with huge aromatic leaves and delicious fruit, adding a tropical feeling to the garden. It needs as much sun as possible and is best grown against a warm wall or in a cool greenhouse. Fig fruits better if the roots are restricted; it is often planted in a large container, which can be sunk in the ground if desired. Plant in a rich mix with plenty of rotted compost and make sure that there is good drainage. Keep well watered and feed with potash, but don't overwater when the fruits are ripening. 'Brown Turkey' is a reliable outdoor variety. 'Brunswick' is a hardy larger fruiting variety, and 'White Marseilles' a hardy pale green variety.

Malus. **Crabapple**. Crabapple is an excellent small tree with fragrant flowers, fall color and little apple fruits that can be made into sumptuous jellies. Blossom ranges from white through to rosy red, fruits from scarlet to gold, and some have fall color. Crabapple is self-fertile and a good pollinator of eating apples. *M. floribunda* is one of the most beautiful ornamental trees with rose buds and pink flowers. 'John Downie' has a profusion of large orange and scarlet fruit.

OPPOSITE **The fruit of a quince scents the air around it, recalling the delights of traditional quince jellies. The flower bud is full of expectation and hope.**

ABOVE LEFT **A fig poses against an unfurling leaf. Figs are magnificent shrubs, with aromatic, architectural leaves; they thrive in a sunny spot.**

ABOVE AND LEFT **Crabapples are regarded as ornamentals, but many have edible fruit. Hybrids include the showy orange and scarlet 'John Downie' to the yellow 'Golden Hornet.' 'John Downie' is a good pollinator of apples.**

RIGHT **Old apple trees are one of the most beautiful sights. Whether in leaf, flower, or fruit, or even bare in winter, they create a wonderful atmosphere.**

OPPOSITE, ABOVE LEFT **Apples that are nearly ripe are irresistible—but, even if they weren't palatable, a tree with fruit as lovely as this would still be planted.**

OPPOSITE, ABOVE RIGHT AND BELOW LEFT **Apples flower like a shower of snow in spring. One of the most reassuring sights of all, it acts as a wake-up call for the gardener.**

OPPOSITE, BELOW RIGHT **The medlar fruit is bizarre, and is difficult to find on sale in a nursery. Quite early in its life, the tree takes on an ancient look, and adds a bit of class to the garden.**

Malus sylvestris var. *domestica*. **Apple**. Apple is the most extensively grown fruit tree and it is easy to understand why. It has soft green leaves and is beautiful in spring, with pink, white, or red-tinged blossom. It fruits gracefully early in life. Apples add a unique charm to a garden in late summer and fall. The range is endless—apples can be trained as espaliers, cordons, or fans, or grown in large containers. 'Cox's Orange Pippin' is a great-tasting apple but very prone to disease. 'Red Falstaff' is quick to fruit, flowers profusely, and is self-fertile. 'Red Devil' is disease-resistant and very easy to grow. Columnar types such as 'North Pole' are good in a small garden. There are so many varieties that the decision about what to grow will depend on personal taste, but try to choose more disease-resistant varieties.

   The rootstocks to look for are:
- Pixie, often used for container growing.
- M27 approximately 4–6ft (1.2–1.8m) when mature.
- M9 approximately 6–8ft (1.8–2.4m) when mature.
- M26 approximately 8–10ft (2.4–3m) when mature.
- MM106 approximately 10–13ft (3–4m) when mature; probably the best for a small garden.

Cooking apples can tolerate some shade, but the best location is sunny and protected from late-spring frosts. Apart from the few self-fertile varieties, apples need a partner that flowers at the same time. There are often pollinators in neighbouring gardens—and apples can also be pollinated by crabapples.

   If you don't have room for more than one tree, and have few other gardens in your neighborhood, the answer may be to purchase a "family tree," which has between two and four different varieties grafted onto it. They can look a bit lopsided since one variety tends to dominate.

   While container-grown plants are available all year, it is best to buy in fall or spring, when fresh stock has arrived at the garden center, or bare-rooted in winter, when the choice is greater and the price is cheaper.

Mespilus germanica. **Medlar**. Medlar makes an enchanting small specimen tree, with its twisting habit, large white flowers and broad leaves that fire up in fall. It is worth cultivating a medlar for its appearance rather than for its strange fruits, which are left to "blet" (partly decompose) before being made into jams. Unfussy, easy, self-pollinating trees, they are happy in any well-drained garden soil. 'Nottingham' is a good, compact variety.

THIS PAGE AND OPPOSITE **A cherry tree in full bloom is an awesome sight, and the fruit, as long as it has been well protected against birds, is delicious straight from the tree. Newer, self-fertile varieties and dwarf rootstocks have made cherries much easier to grow in a garden with limited space.**

Morus spp. **Mulberry**. The classical dome-shaped mulberry with its broad heart-shaped leaves, and golden fall color, looks aristocratic on an open lawn. When mature it has a wonderful gnarled trunk. Harvesting the loganberry-like fruits is done by shaking the branches onto a sheet or newspapers while trying to avoid getting covered in the staining juices of the falling fruits. The fruit, which are rarely available in markets, are delicious, both sweet and sharp. The black mulberry (*M. nigra*) is the best for fruit. When planting, take care not to damage the brittle roots. Only prune if essential because the wood "bleeds." They can be grown as bushes, but this seems rather a shame.

Prunus armeniaca. **Apricot**. Apricot is lovely in flower and particularly beautiful when trained on a wall. But it is quite difficult to grow. It needs a cold winter to rest, an early spring so that the flowers don't get caught by frost, and a long summer for the fruit to ripen. Unless the climate is reliable, grow under glass, train against a sunny wall, or grow in pots outside bringing them in while in flower and until the weather warms up. The best rootstock for training is St Julien A. Apricots are self-pollinating, so you only need one tree for fruit. 'Moorpark' has a great flavor.

Prunus avium. **Cherry**. A full-blown sweet cherry covered in white blossom or with its fall hues is a sight to behold. Added to that is the wonderful spectacle of the tree dripping with cherries. But the blossom comes early and is sensitive to frost, and the fruit draws birds like a magnet. For a small garden, look for plants grown on Colt or the extremely dwarf Tabel rootstock. 'Stella' and 'Celeste' are self-fertile sweet cherries with excellent-flavored fruit and don't grow too big. Cherries grown as trees do not need to be pruned except to remove damaged and diseased branches. The cooking

91

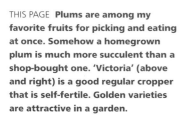

THIS PAGE **Plums are among my favorite fruits for picking and eating at once. Somehow a homegrown plum is much more succulent than a shop-bought one. 'Victoria' (above and right) is a good regular cropper that is self-fertile. Golden varieties are attractive in a garden.**

varieties such as 'Morello' (*P. cerasus*) are easier to grow. They are self-fertile and enjoy shade, thriving against a north-facing wall. Protect from birds with bird netting.

Prunus domestica. **Plum**. The plum tree is a spectacular flowering tree in spring, with a slightly weeping habit. In winter the bare tree can look a little gloomy. There are plenty of self-fertile varieties such as the excellent 'Victoria', which will also take some shade. For a small tree go for Pixie rootstock, and St Julien A for a larger one. 'Jubileum' is quite

With its slightly weeping habit, the blossom-covered plum tree is spectacular in spring.

disease-resistant and has fruit with a good flavor. If you live in a cold climate, look for a late-flowering variety. Plums like quite a heavy soil so will tolerate clay soils. Greengage plums are quite delicious when picked and eaten straight from the tree. They require slightly more warmth than plums and have less ornamental value. 'Oulins Golden Gage' has beautiful golden-yellow fruit.

Prunus insititia. **Damson plum**. Damson plums are more compact than other plums and have a spicier flavor. They are hardier, fruit later and are usually grown as large informal bushes or small wide trees. Lovely in flower, mostly self-fertile with beautiful blush blue fruit. They make an excellent windbreak and can take some shade. 'Merryweather' has larger fruit, and 'Shropshire' has a very good flavor

THIS PAGE **My mother used to cook wonderful damson plum desserts made from the fruit of a large tree in our neighbor's garden, so the sight of this harvest brings back happy memories. Damson plum trees are hardy and easy to grow.**

THIS PAGE, ABOVE LEFT AND RIGHT
The best place for peaches is under cover or against a wall. Growing peaches in a greenhouse will protect them against leaf curl, and the fruit will ripen better, particularly in cooler climates.

THIS PAGE, LEFT AND FAR LEFT **Nectarines are similar to peaches but without the downy skin. Since they are less hardy, they need to be given some shelter to thrive.**

OPPOSITE **Full of character in winter with wizened bark, spectacular in flower, and producing succulent and delicious fruit, the pear is a great fruit tree. Choosing appropriate varieties is important—my father's pears tasted sweet and juicy but had a texture like iron. It is worth trying one or two older types.**

Prunus persica. **Peach** and **nectarine**. Peach is a lovely tree for a small garden. It has delicate pink blossom in spring and beautiful fruit in summer. But peach leaf-curl is so disfiguring and common that it is hard to recommend peaches wholeheartedly. The spores are carried in the rain, so, to protect the plants, encase them in a plastic cover from midwinter to spring when the new leaves appear. Although they are self-pollinating, they flower before there is much bee activity. Help pollination by gently tapping or shaking the branches when in flower, or hand pollinate by transferring pollen from one flower to another with a small soft brush. 'Peregrine', 'Duke of York,' and 'Rochester' are reliable varieties.

Nectarines are something of a gamble to grow outside in cooler climates. Cultivation is the same for both, though nectarines need even more warmth and are the less productive of the two. Both grow well in pots, especially if they can be brought in at crucial times. Otherwise grow against a sheltered south-facing wall.

Pyrus communis var. *sativa*. **Pear**. Mature pear trees are one of the most beautiful specimen trees to have in a garden. They have a fissured bark that gives the impression of great age and wisdom. Their white flowers sparkle in the spring sunshine, and the developing fruit looks like baubles on a Christmas tree, just waiting for the ripe moment. They flower earlier than apples so need to be sited in a sheltered sunny spot, away from easterly winds. Pears are usually grafted onto quince rootstocks known as Quince A, which will grow no higher than 20ft (6m), and Quince C, which is a little smaller and tends to need good conditions. Pears take pruning well and can be manipulated into any shape. They enjoy the warmth of a wall, making them good subjects for training flat. There are few self-pollinators, so, if space is a problem, a row of cordons could be the answer. 'Doyenne du Comice' bears heavy crops of sweet and delicious fruit, 'Beth' is small and compact, and 'Concorde' is self-fertile and compact. Newer varieties are also more disease-resistant.

berries and small fruits

The contrast between freshly picked soft fruit from the garden and the store-bought variety is huge. Compare the flavor of home-grown alpine or wild strawberries with the watery flavor of the giant beasts bought in a basket. Make space for a few small fruits and taste the difference.

Fragaria spp. **Strawberry**. Strawberries are the very essence of summer. They are simple to grow in the garden or in containers. Alpine and wild strawberries produce delicious small tangy fruit, and the hybrids are larger and glossier. I think the alpines are better for a mixed garden since they can tolerate some shade and are ideal for underplanting, edging and look lovely mixed in with geraniums, lady's mantle, violas, and primroses. They also grow well in containers and hanging baskets. Beware of slugs and snails. The everbearing types fruit a second time in late summer. There can often be problems with disease, so it is best to renew plants every 3–4 years and plant in a different location annually.

Rheum x *cultorum*. **Rhubarb**. Rhubarb is a majestic ornamental with huge creased handsome leaves, red-tinged stems and powerful thrusting flowers in the summer. They look great with other large-leaved plants and do well in partial shade. It is not only the earliest 'fruit' of the year but the easiest and most reliable. Plant with plenty of well-rotted manure because they are greedy feeders and they're going to stay a long time. For earliest rhubarb cover with straw and a rhubarb 'forcer' (or a bottomless bucket) in late winter. When harvesting, twist the stems, don't cut them.

Ribes nigrum. **Black currant**. Black currant bushes look wonderful when dripping with ripe fruit. Their foliage is a fresh green and they mix well in a border. Black currants can take a little shade but fruit better in sun. Greedy feeders, they need rich moisture-retentive soil, and plenty of mulching and feed. Buy an established plant in fall. Protect from birds when the fruits form. Black currants fruit on the previous year's wood so cut those that have fruited and leave the pale, younger stems that sprung last summer to fruit in the next. 'Ben Sarek' is good for a small garden and is mildew-resistant; 'Ben Connan' has a good flavor.

OPPOSITE **Strawberries are among the easiest fruits to grow, though slugs need to be kept at bay. Straw can protect the fruit from damage by direct contact with the soil, help reduce slug damage and stop soil splash. Strawberry flowers are a cheering sight in the season.**

LEFT, ABOVE AND BELOW **The rhubarb plant has one of the most majestic leaves in the garden. There are some purely ornamental members of the family, but the edible form is no less attractive. Rhubarb makes a substantial and confident clump in a border.**

BELOW **Black currants resemble little black jewels, and are best eaten right away. Protect from birds with bird netting.**

SOFT FRUIT

THIS PAGE AND OPPOSITE, ABOVE LEFT
Red currant fruits look beautiful when just starting to ripen as well as when fully mature; they are also irresistible to birds.

OPPOSITE, ABOVE CENTER AND RIGHT
Blackberries are well worth planting at the back of a garden. I like their informality and wildness, which can be used to soften hard edges. The gradual ripening of blackberries extends the picking season.

OPPOSITE, BELOW LEFT AND CENTER
Gooseberries are at home in an informal setting and look playful when in fruit. In a good year, a couple of bushes will give a plentiful crop. A tree-form gooseberry adds a bit of height to a border.

OPPOSITE, BELOW RIGHT **Rich in flavor when fully ripe, loganberries can provide an excellent yield.**

Ribes sativum. **Red currant** and **white currant**. Red currants and white currants are beautiful in the garden, with handsome leaves and delicate bunches of scarlet or white berries. They can take partial shade and grow well on a north wall. Prune lightly in summer and harder in winter, leaving the old framework and the leaders while shortening new growths to keep the plant looking tidy.

Ribes uva-crispa. **Gooseberry**. As a bush, gooseberries are quite messy; however, when grown as a standard, they are both more decorative and more manageable. It is vital to choose mildew-resistant varieties such as 'Invicta', 'Pax Red,' and 'Oregon Champion'. Gooseberries like a well-drained soil that holds the moisture well, so incorporate plenty of organic matter. Don't let them dry out. They prefer a little shade in the height of summer. A slight breeze improves air circulation controls mildew.

Rubus fruticosus. **Blackberry**. Blackberries are considered by many to be more suited to keep out vandals than for growing as a fruit crop in a civilized garden. The new tamer varieties have transformed blackberry growing. 'Oregon Thornless,' with its divided leaves and fall color, is an extremely ornamental climber. 'Ashton Cross' tastes as good as the wild blackberry. Blackberries are easy to grow and provide the last berries of the season. They flower late—which avoids the frost problem—and they tolerate shade, although they ripen more sweetly in the sun. Plant bare-rooted canes in early spring in soil with plenty of organic matter. Provide sturdy supports and cut off all the canes that have fruited after harvest.

Rubus hybrids. **Loganberry** and **raspberry/blackberry** crosses. Loganberries and the numerous raspberry/blackberry crosses have been bred for taste. They have the same prickly, rampant tendencies as blackberries and are not particularly ornamental. Treat in the same way as blackberries. The fruit is long and juicy and makes superlative jam. The LY59 is thornless with more moderate habits.

Rubus idaeus. **Raspberry**. Although not particularly ornamental until in fruit, fresh raspberries are incomparable to store-bought ones, and are rewarding and uncomplicated for the kitchen gardener. They like cool moist conditions and don't mind a little shade. Plant canes in fall no more than 3in (7.5cm) deep. Support and protect against birds.

Prune summer raspberries in fall by cutting out all the canes that have fruited, while leaving the strongest new unfruited canes for next year's crop. Prune fall raspberries by cutting off all the old fruited canes in late winter. Tie in the new ones as they grow during the following spring and summer. 'Autumn Bliss' is a reliable late cropper, and 'Boyne' and 'Meeker' are large with a good flavor.

Vaccinium corymbosum and *Vaccinium oxycoccos*. **Blueberry** and **cranberry**. An eye-catching shrub when thriving, with wonderful fall color, blueberry tends to look rather despondent and desperate in the wrong conditions. Blueberries will thrive in moist, acidic soil. A pH lower than 5.5 is best. Though self-pollinating, they fruit better when more than one variety is planted. Excellent varieties include 'Blue Crop' and 'Patriot.'

Cranberry is a specialty crop that requires moist or semi-boggy conditions. For cranberry to thrive in a garden, the soil needs to be even more acid than for blueberries.

Vitis vinifera. **Grapevine**. Grapes are among the most glorious of vines. They combine fine leaves, gorgeous fruit and a bark that becomes fascinating and gnarled, so that even in winter, a vine can add real character to the garden. In a mild climate the fruit often fails to sweeten. They fruit more reliably under cover in cool climates.

Grapes need plenty of sunlight, a warm and airy spot and—if grown outside—the protection of a wall. They like free-draining rich soil. The main disease problem is mildew. 'Brandt' is hardy and vigorous, with a wonderful display of fall color, and small black miniature bunches, 'Boskoop Glory' is a good dark grape, and 'Elenora' is a spicy blue that is mildew-resistant. The work comes in the pruning. First there is the formative pruning to get the right framework. This can take a couple of years and is often done along horizontal wires for even fruiting. In summer the shoots are trimmed to three or four leaves beyond the flowers and all extraneous growths are removed.

Grapes can be grown successfully in containers with even harsher pruning, but it is important to make sure that container-grown plants never dry out.

OPPOSITE, TOP ROW **One of the best sights in the season is ripening raspberries, somehow summing up the essence of the kitchen garden. Raspberries are easy to grow, and yummy when fresh. Young children (up to the age of 50) will strip the plant before you know it. A golden raspberry is a decorative variation.**

ABOVE **Cranberries are only worth growing if you have a moist, acidic soil, and they need to be kept well watered.**

LEFT **Blueberries can be quite tricky, though in the right conditions they grow well, and their taste when fresh is in a class of its own.**

RIGHT AND FAR RIGHT **Grapes are highly desirable garden plants. They are great climbers, with good foliage and beautiful fruit. Some of the newer varieties are more disease-resistant and tend to fruit better in a temperate climate.**

LEFT **The foliage of the kiwi fruit is magnificent but climbs at great speed.**

BELOW LEFT **Oranges and other citrus fruits need consistent warmth to thrive. In most climates they will grow in a greenhouse or conservatory.**

OPPOSITE **A heated melon house such as this one is not something that most people would have room to accommodate in their gardens, but this partly sunken greenhouse provides the ideal conditions for a spectacular crop of melons.**

tender fruit

The thought of growing an orange or lemon in your garden may seem far-fetched in a cool climate, but—as long as you can protect these tender plants from the cold—the flowers alone are so wonderfully scented that any fruit is a delightful bonus.

Actinidia deliciosa. **Kiwi**. Kiwi fruits are exotic-looking climbers with heart-shaped leaves and rosy white flowers. Too vigorous for most greenhouses, they are best grown outside in a sheltered warm spot. They don't bear fruit for about four years and only after a long hot summer. Treat in the same way as grapevines. A reliable variety is 'Hayward', which will need a male partner planted within 16ft (5m).

Citrus spp. **Orange** and **lemon**. Oranges and lemons are frost tender. They have gloriously scented flowers and aromatic leaves. They grow very well in containers, bringing a touch of classical Italian elegance to a conservatory or can they live in a warm garden as long as they are brought in during chilly spells. The minimum temperature in winter is 50°F (10°C). Plant in slightly acidic soil that has been mixed with some coarse sand. Good drainage is vital. Keep regularly watered. Feed with a high-nitrogen fertilizer through summer and a good well-balanced fertilizer with trace elements through winter. Prune only if the plant becomes untidy.

Cucumis melo. **Melon**. Annual. Melons are a tender crop traditionally raised in a heated greenhouse. New quick-growing varieties, including the cantaloupes 'Ogen' and 'Sweetheart', have made it possible to grow them in a cold frame outside in temperate climates. Melons are grown in the same way as cucumbers. Pinch out the side shoots when they have produced three leaves to encourage fruiting. The fruits benefit from being put into net 'slings' as they become heavy.

Passiflora edulis. **Passion fruit**. Passion fruit looks much like the stunning passionflower. It has glorious white flowers with purple centers and handsome serrated leaves. To grow the exotic-tasting fruits, you need a long warm summer or a greenhouse. Passion fruits are grown in the same way as kiwis, but unlike kiwis, they are self-pollinating.

vegetarian recipes for
herbs, vegetables, and fruit

soups and appetizers

celery and tarragon soup

The flavor of celery grows stronger closer to its heart, so use as much of it as possible, as well as the leaves. In this soup the sweet tang of apple juice complements the aniseed taste, while bringing out the celery's earthiness.

2 tablespoons extra virgin olive oil
2 onions, chopped
1lb (400g) celery, cleaned and chopped
2 garlic cloves, chopped
2 cups (500ml) apple juice
a large handful of fresh tarragon, leaves
    stripped, chopped
sea salt and freshly ground black pepper
thick yogurt, to serve
Serves 4

Heat the olive oil in a saucepan over medium heat. Add the onion and celery and sauté gently until softened, but not browned. Add the garlic and cook for about 1–2 minutes until fragrant. Pour in the apple juice and 2 cups (500ml) water. Season generously with salt and pepper.

Reserve a little tarragon for serving and add the remainder to the soup. Simmer for 10 minutes. Using a hand-held blender, purée the soup until smooth. Serve in warmed bowls with a spoonful of yogurt and the reserved tarragon.

chilled lettuce soup

Cold, clean-tasting soups are a great way to start a meal—although they only appeal when the weather is very warm. Avoid using lettuce that has bolted or is oozing a milky substance from the stem, which may give a bitter taste. For best results, all the ingredients should be cold before you start. This means that less chilling time is required and the lettuce will keep its crunch.

½ lb (250g) lettuce, cleaned and chopped
2 cups (250g) yogurt
1 small garlic clove, crushed with a pinch of
    coarse salt
1in (1–2cm) long piece of fresh ginger, peeled
    and finely grated
fresh mint leaves
juice of ½ lemon
sea salt and freshly ground black pepper
Serves 4

Put all the ingredients in a food processor or blender, adding just enough water to get the blades moving, and blend until the desired consistency is achieved. Blending time varies according to the type of lettuce and the type of machine you are using, but aim to make the soup fairly smooth.

tomato and ginger soup

This velvety sweet broth buzzing with ginger needs lots of tomatoes but hardly any work. Just put it all in a saucepan and rub through a mesh strainer at the end. For a thick soup, use less liquid.

3lb (1.25kg) ripe tomatoes
3 cups (600ml) vegetable broth or water
1oz (30g) piece of fresh ginger, peeled and
    coarsely chopped
4 garlic cloves, coarsely chopped
1 tablespoon dark brown sugar, or to taste
sea salt and freshly ground black pepper
chopped fresh parsley, to serve
Serves 4–6

Put the tomatoes in a saucepan, add the broth, cover, bring to a boil, then lower the heat to a gentle simmer. Cook for 10 minutes, then add the ginger, garlic, and sugar. Season with salt and pepper, and stir well. Cover and simmer for 30 minutes.

Remove the saucepan from the heat and let it cool slightly. Using a hand-held blender, purée the soup until smooth, then press through a strainer into a clean saucepan. Test seasoning and reheat gently until piping hot. Ladle into warmed cups or bowls and serve.

celery and tarragon soup

little parcels of goat cheese and plums

little parcels of goat cheese and plums

Try these appealing little parcels—warm cheese and sweet plums with a touch of fennel—as a first course, served with a few wild leaves or herbs trickled with olive oil. If you use mature goat cheese, make sure it is to everyone's taste—it is safer to choose a soft, mild one or use cream cheese as an alternative.

8oz (125g) filo pastry
½ stick (50g) salted butter, melted
8oz (125g) goat cheese, divided into 8 portions
4 plums, halved and stoned
1 tablespoon fennel seeds
2 tablespoons chopped fresh fennel leaves
freshly ground black pepper

a large cookie sheet, greased
Makes 8 small parcels

Cut the pastry into 16 pieces, each about 6in (15cm) square. Keep the pastry covered with a damp dishtowel while you work. Put a square of pastry on the work surface and brush with a little melted butter. Put a second square on top, rotating it 45 degrees, and brush with melted butter. Put the goat cheese in the center, top with half a plum, and sprinkle with pepper and a few fennel seeds and leaves. Gather up the edges around the filling and press together at the top. Put the parcels on the prepared cookie sheet and brush the outsides with more butter.

When the parcels are ready, they can be stored, covered, in the refrigerator for up to 2 hours. Bake on the lower shelf of a preheated oven at 425°F (220°C) for 10–15 minutes until golden, then serve.

galette of pears and blue cheese

Pears and blue cheese go terrifically well together. This recipe frames their winning partnership in puff pastry. Simple as that—easy, pretty, and delicious. For the flakiest texture, use all-butter puff pastry.

2 small pears
4–6oz (150–200g) puff pastry
4oz (100g) blue cheese, such as Roquefort, crumbled
a little melted butter

a large cookie sheet, greased
Serves 4

Peel the pears with a vegetable peeler, then cut the pears in half and scoop out the core from the base, leaving the top intact. Finely slice each half lengthwise, leaving it attached at the stem end, then spread carefully into a fan shape. Set aside until required.

Put the pastry on a work surface and roll out to ¼ in (5mm) thick, then cut into 4 rectangles, each at least ½ in (1cm) longer and ½ in (1cm) wider than the pears. Arrange the rectangles on the cookie sheet and top each one with cheese. Using a palette knife, put the pear fans on top of the cheese and brush all over with melted butter. Bake in a preheated oven at 425°F (220°C) for 15–20 minutes until the pastry is puffed and golden. Serve warm.

white bean and roasted garlic purée

A creamy cousin of humus, this purée is pale and delicate, yet rich and satisfying. Roasting the garlic mellows its vigor and creates a caramel tone. Cannellini beans have a superb flavor, but haricot or butter beans are good, too. This is a rare case in which canned beans are not a satisfactory substitute.

½ lb (125g) dried cannellini beans
5–6 bay leaves
1 large head of garlic
2–3 tablespoons extra virgin olive oil
juice of 1 lemon
sea salt and freshly ground black pepper
cayenne pepper
Serves 4–8

Put the beans in a large bowl and pour in plenty of water to cover. Soak overnight. Drain and rinse the beans thoroughly, then put them in a large pan and cover with at least twice their volume of cold water.

Add the bay leaves and bring to a boil over medium heat. Boil rapidly for 10–15 minutes, skimming off any foam with a slotted spoon. Lower the heat, add a little salt, and simmer until the beans are tender, about 40–50 minutes. When cooked, the beans should be very tender. Strain the beans, reserving the cooking liquid; then let the beans and liquid cool.

Slice the top off the garlic bulb and put the head in a small roasting pan. Roast in a preheated oven at 400°F (200°C) for 30 minutes. Remove from the oven, let it cool, then peel the garlic cloves.

Put the beans and garlic in a food processor and process until smooth, adding a little reserved cooking water until a smooth paste is formed. Work in the olive oil, lemon juice, pepper, and salt if necessary.

Spoon the mixture into a bowl and, using the back of a spoon, smooth the surface. Trickle on a little olive oil, dust with cayenne, and serve.

basil and chile labne

Labne is a soft, creamy cheese made from strained yogurt. Much of the fun of cooking comes from watching food change as you apply various forces to it—and this is a perfect example, using the force of gravity. I love the sharp, clean combination of basil and chile, but you can experiment with other herbs and whole spices, such as cilantro and cumin seeds.

4 cups (400ml) full-fat natural yogurt
1 fresh red chile, chopped
10–12 fresh basil leaves, chopped
grated zest of 1 lemon
pinch of salt
extra virgin olive oil
a few drops of balsamic vinegar

TO SERVE
warm bread
crunchy raw vegetables

a large serving plate, lightly oiled
Serves 4

Line a fine strainer with a clean kitchen cloth or cheesecloth and set it over a deep bowl so there is plenty of space for the whey to drain away.

Put the yogurt, chile, basil, lemon zest, and salt into a large bowl and mix thoroughly. Scoop the mixture into the cloth and press down with a spoon. Chill in the refrigerator for 24–36 hours.

Invert the labne onto the prepared serving plate and trickle on olive oil and a few drops of balsamic vinegar. For a gorgeous presentation, use wet hands to roll the labne into balls, then put them on the prepared plate. Trickle on more olive oil and vinegar. Chill in the refrigerator until ready to eat. Serve with warm bread and crunchy raw vegetables.

basil and chile labne

main courses

asparagus flan

Don't be scared by the pastry case—it is easy to make in a food processor. The secret to light, flaky pastry is to handle it as little as possible—don't knead, just press into a slab. This flan makes a classy lunch or picnic dish.

PASTRY

1²/₃ cups (200g) plain flour

pinch of sea salt

1 stick (100g) very cold butter, cubed

1 teaspoon fennel seeds (optional)

1 egg yolk mixed with
2 tablespoons iced water

FILLING

350g asparagus spears

3 egg yolks

¾ cup (150g) crème fraîche or soured cream

sea salt and freshly ground black pepper

2 tablespoons (25g) Parmesan cheese, freshly grated

fluted pie plate with removable base

Serves 4–6

To make the pastry, put the flour in a food processor, add a pinch of salt. and pulse a few times to aerate. Add the butter and the fennel seeds, if using, and process until the mixture resembles fine breadcrumbs. Gradually add the egg yolk and water, and pulse until the pastry just begins to pull together. (Overprocessing results in tough pastry.) Turn the dough out onto a clean work surface, press into a slab, cover with plastic wrap, and chill in the refrigerator for about 30 minutes.

Roll out the dough on a lightly floured work surface, taking care that it doesn't stick to the surface, and redusting underneath. Roll the dough up onto the rolling pin and lay in the fluted pie plate. Press the dough into the sides of the plate and trim with a knife. Press the sides in again so they extend slightly beyond the edge to allow for shrinkage. Set aside any extra dough for patching up cracks in the case once it is baked. Put the case in the freezer. It must be very cold or—even better—frozen when it goes into the oven.

Line the pastry case with baking parchment and fill with baking beans, pasta, or rice. Bake in a preheated oven at 350°F (180°C) for 10 minutes. Remove the baking parchment and beans, and bake for a further 10 minutes. Patch up any holes or cracks with the extra dough.

To make the filling, bring a saucepan of salted water to a boil. Snap the tough ends off the asparagus and blanch the spears for 3 minutes or until just tender. Drain and refresh under cold running water until cool. Slice off the tips, plus an extra inch or two, and set aside.

Chop the remaining asparagus and put it in a food processor. Add the egg yolks, crème fraîche, salt, and pepper and process until a smooth purée forms. Pour into the pastry case, arrange the reserved tips on top and sprinkle with Parmesan. Bake in the preheated oven for 30 minutes or until golden on top. Remove from the oven and let it cool. When cool, remove from the pie plate, cut into wedges, and serve.

onion, sage, and red wine risotto

The blushing, creamy, al dente risotto rice contrasts nicely with the melting onions and balmy sage. Use carnaroli risotto rice for the best flavor. This risotto has a home-cooked feel to it, though the fried sage gives it dinner-party flair.

4 cups (1 litre) vegetable broth
3 tablespoons extra virgin olive oil
1½ lb (600g) onions, thickly sliced
1¾ cups (350g) risotto rice
20–30 young fresh sage leaves, chopped
3 cups (300ml) full-bodied red wine
2oz (50g) Parmesan cheese, freshly grated, plus extra to serve
20 fresh sage leaves, to serve

Serves 4

Put the broth in a saucepan and heat gently. Heat 2 tablespoons of olive oil in a heavy-based saucepan over low to medium heat. Add the onions and sauté until golden and softened. Increase the heat slightly, add the rice and stir, using a wooden spoon, until the grains are golden and slightly translucent. Add the chopped sage, then pour in the wine. Season to taste with salt and pepper, and stir frequently until all the wine is absorbed. Add a ladle of hot broth, stirring constantly, until it has been absorbed. Continue to add the broth at intervals and cook as before until all the liquid is absorbed and the rice is tender but still slightly firm to the bite. Stir in the grated Parmesan cheese, cover, and let it rest for 2–3 minutes.

Meanwhile, make the garnish. Heat the remaining oil in a stove-top grill pan over high heat. Add the sage leaves and fry briskly until crisp.

Transfer the risotto to 4 warmed plates and top with fried sage and oil, and extra grated Parmesan.

cabbage gratin

A classic gratin is made using a heart-stopping quantity of cream and cheese. This crust is made from yogurt and a little cheese, making it is easier on the heart and waistline. Marmalade adds a citrus zing, which complements the cabbage.

1 tablespoon extra virgin olive oil
3 garlic cloves, chopped
1 medium-sized (600g) cabbage, shredded
2 tablespoons orange marmalade
3 cups (400ml) low-fat yogurt
3 egg yolks
2oz (50g) Cheddar cheese, grated
fresh thyme sprigs, leaves stripped
1 teaspoon caraway seeds
sea salt and freshly ground black pepper

a large ovenproof dish

Serves 4

Heat the olive oil in a saucepan over low heat. Add the garlic and sauté until lightly golden. Add the cabbage and season well with salt and pepper. Cover and cook, stirring frequently, until the cabbage is tender, about 15 minutes.

Remove the saucepan from the heat. If there is juice in the pan, pour it away, then spoon the cabbage into a large ovenproof dish and pack it down. Brush the marmalade over the surface of the cabbage.

Put the yogurt, egg yolks, cheese, thyme, and a pinch of salt in a large mixing bowl and, using a wooden spoon, beat together. Pour the mixture over the cabbage and sprinkle with caraway seeds. Bake in a preheated oven at 400°F (200°C) for 30–40 minutes until the top is golden and bubbling around the edges. Serve.

onion, sage, and red wine risotto

spinach with bulgar wheat and tahini dressing

spinach with bulgar wheat and tahini dressing

This dish is reminiscent of the cuisine of the Mideast, where bulgar or cracked wheat is consumed in many guises. Any green vegetable is suitable—try chard, sorrel, arugula, or leaf beet instead of spinach. If bulgar wheat is not available, use couscous.

¾ cup (150g) bulgar wheat
2 tablespoons extra virgin olive oil
2 onions, sliced
½ lb (150g) spinach or other greens, cleaned and
   coarsely chopped
2 tablespoons tahini (sesame paste)
1 garlic clove, crushed
juice of 1 lemon
2 tablespoons yogurt
sea salt and freshly ground black pepper
2 tablespoons toasted pinola
Serves 4

Put the bulgar wheat into a bowl and pour in enough boiling water to cover. Let it swell for 20 minutes, then drain if necessary. Separate the grains with a fork.

Heat the oil in a saucepan over medium heat. Add the onions and sauté until softened and golden. Stir in the bulgar wheat and spinach, then cover and cook until the spinach is just wilted.

Put the tahini, 4 tablespoons of hot water, garlic, lemon juice, and yogurt in a large bowl. Season with salt and pepper and stir together until smooth. Transfer the spinach mixture to a large serving dish and spoon on the tahini dressing. Sprinkle the top with toasted pinola and serve.

linguine with sage and walnut pesto

This pesto needs a lot of sage, and the waxiness of the herb makes it much drier than basil pesto. Try it with any pasta, but strappy linguine carry the sticky pesto well. You can multiply the quantities and keep the pesto in a jar in the refrigerator for up to 2 weeks, covered by a film of olive oil.

¾ cup (75g) walnuts
fresh sage leaves, about 2 large handfuls
4 tablespoons (50g) Parmesan cheese, freshly grated
2 garlic cloves, chopped
juice and grated zest of ½ lemon
5 tablespoons extra virgin olive oil
1 lb (500g) fresh linguine
sea salt and freshly ground black pepper

a large baking sheet
Serves 4–6

Put the walnuts on a large baking sheet and toast them in a preheated oven at 400°F (200°C) for about 5 minutes, or until their color deepens. Remove from the oven and let cool.

Put the walnuts, sage, Parmesan, garlic, lemon juice and rind and zest, and pepper in a spice grinder, food processor, or mortar and process or pound until a medium-coarse paste forms.

Bring a large saucepan of salted water to a boil over medium heat. As soon as it comes to a rolling boil, add a dash of olive oil and drop in the linguine. Return to a boil and cook, stirring frequently, until al dente or still firm to the bite, about 6–7 minutes. Drain, but not too well—a slight moisture will help to distribute the pesto. Return the pasta to the saucepan and, using 2 wooden spoons or spaghetti forks, toss the pesto through the linguine until evenly coated. Serve immediately.

creamy cauliflower and couscous roast

Cauliflower and cheese make a great team, but this recipe is a departure from the standard dish. It is much lighter, but still creamy, and the crunchy couscous and caper crust make it a meal in itself—ideal for a simple, comforting winter supper.

2 cups (250ml) white wine

1 cauliflower, cut into
   small florets

2 teaspoons wholegrain mustard

¼ stick (25g) butter

1 cup (200g) couscous

½ cup (125g) milk

6oz (200g) light cream cheese,
   cut into pieces

2 tablespoons capers, rinsed

4oz (100g) Gruyère cheese, grated

a handful of fresh chives, snipped

sea salt

cayenne pepper

a large ovenproof dish

Serves 4

Put the wine and 2 cups (250ml) water in a large saucepan and bring to a boil over medium heat. Add the cauliflower and a pinch of salt, return to a boil, then reduce to a simmer. Cover with a lid and poach for 5 minutes or until the cauliflower is just tender.

Strain the cauliflower into a bowl, reserving the liquid, then beat the mustard and butter into the liquid. Put the couscous into another bowl, pour the liquid on the couscous, and let it soak for about 5 minutes. Arrange the cauliflower in a single layer in an ovenproof dish.

Put the milk in a saucepan and heat until almost boiling. Beat in the cream cheese to form a thick sauce, then pour it on the cauliflower.

Fluff up the soaked couscous with a fork, then stir in the capers, Gruyère, and chives. Spoon the couscous mixture on the cauliflower, sprinkle with cayenne, and bake in a preheated oven at 400° (200°C) for 30–40 minutes until golden. Serve immediately.

pumpkin and cilantro curry

This Thai-style curry sings with flavor. Although the spicy paste makes even a bland vegetable palatable, a sweet, densely textured pumpkin, or squash such as butternut or acorn, is ideal. Use fresh cilantro (coriander) seeds if you can; they have a fabulous perfume, as do the roots and stems. The stems can also be used to make a tasty broth, along with leek greens.

2 tablespoons vegetable oil

2lb (1kg) pumpkin, cut into
   1in (2cm) chunks

4 leeks, cleaned and chopped

2½ cups (300ml) coconut milk

2 cups (250ml) broth made from
   leek greens and cilantro stems,
   or 2 cups (250ml) water

5 kaffir lime leaves (optional)

sea salt and freshly ground black
   pepper

boiled rice, to serve

CURRY PASTE

1 large handful of fresh cilantro,
   including leaves, seeds, stems,
   and roots

4 large garlic cloves

2in (5 cm) long piece of fresh
   ginger, peeled

1 teaspoon dried chile flakes or
   1 fresh chile

1 teaspoon sea salt

Serves 4

To make the curry paste, put all the ingredients in a blender, adding just enough water to let the blades move, and process until smooth.

Put the vegetable oil in a wide, heavy-based stove-top grill pan and heat well. Add the pumpkin, leeks, and a pinch of salt and sauté gently until the leeks have softened. Stir in the paste and fry for 2–3 minutes. Add the coconut milk, broth, and lime leaves, if using, then season to taste with salt and pepper. Bring the mixture to a boil, then lower the heat and simmer until the pumpkin is very soft. To thicken the curry, mash several pieces of pumpkin with a fork and stir through the gravy. Serve with boiled rice.

pumpkin and cilantro curry

salads and light dishes

broccoli salad with sugared sunflower seeds

Very finely chopped raw broccoli is totally different from the cooked vegetable. Don't throw away the trunklike stalk. Shave off the outside "bark" and use the sweet, pale flesh inside.

3 tablespoons sunflower seeds
2 teaspooons unrefined sugar
½ lb (300g) broccoli
juice of 1 lemon

2 tablespoons extra virgin olive oil
sea salt and freshly ground black
   pepper
Serves 4

Heat a non-stick grill pan over medium heat. Toss the sunflower seeds in the pan and sprinkle the sugar over them. Cook, stirring frequently, until the sugar melts, coats the seeds, and they turn golden. Transfer the seeds to a plate and let them cool. Break them up if they clump together.

Break the broccoli into pieces, then put it in a food processor and chop very finely. Alternatively, grate the broccoli on the coarse side of a grater into a bowl. Put the broccoli in a serving bowl and add the lemon juice and olive oil. Season well with salt and pepper, and stir until mixed. Stir in the sugared seeds and serve.

honey-roasted zucchini and feta

Zucchini and feta cheese share a love of being roasted—they both take on a lovely chewy texture. Trickling them with honey intensifies this effect and gives a superb contrasting flavor to the tangy cheese. Small zucchini usually have the best flavor, but large ones work well, too.

1lb (500g) zucchini, deseeded if large, cut into chunky strips
2 garlic cloves, sliced
3 tablespoons extra virgin olive oil
8oz (200g) feta cheese, coarsely crumbled
2 tablespoons runny honey
freshly ground black pepper

a large ovenproof dish
Serves 4

Put the zucchini in a large ovenproof dish in a single layer. Add the garlic and sprinkle with 2 tablespoons of olive oil. Using your hands, toss the zucchini until they are evenly coated with the garlic and oil.

Spread out the zucchini evenly in the dish. Scatter the feta cheese over them and trickle on the remaining olive oil, honey, and pepper. The saltiness of the feta means that no extra salt is needed. Roast in a preheated oven at 425°F (220°C) for 20–30 minutes until deep golden all over. Transfer to a serving dish and serve immediately.

warm salad of green beans, dill, and thyme

This herby salad dressing seems to bring out the best in any podded beans. You can turn the salad into a complete meal by serving it on baked potatoes.

1lb (250g) green beans, cut into
   1in (2cm) pieces
1 cup (200g) natural yogurt
finely grated zest of ½ lemon
juice of 1 lemon
a handful of fresh dill, chopped
3 fresh thyme sprigs, leaves stripped
1 small garlic clove, crushed
sea salt and freshly ground black pepper

a large steamer
Serves 4

Put the green beans in a steamer set over a saucepan of gently simmering water and steam until tender.

Put the remaining ingredients in a large bowl and beat together. Mix through the steamed beans while still warm and serve immediately.

crushed potato and arugula salad

The simplest and best potato salad lets the true flavor of the potato shine through—and nothing tastes quite as sweet and earthy as a freshly dug organic potato from your garden. Floury potatoes will behave differently from waxy ones—either works well, but a floury variety is preferable. Watercress can be used instead of arugula.

2lb (1kg) potatoes, cut in large chunks
2 tablespoons red wine vinegar
½ cup (50g) arugula leaves
2 tablespoons extra virgin olive oil
sea salt and freshly ground black pepper
Serves 4

Bring a large saucepan of lightly salted water to a boil over medium heat. Add the potatoes and cook until tender. Drain and put the potatoes in a large bowl and, using a fork, crush lightly so they are chunky rather than mashed. Sprinkle the vinegar on the potatoes and let them cool without stirring.

When completely cool, add the arugula, olive oil, and salt and pepper to the potatoes and gently toss until mixed. Serve immediately.

orange, radish, and carrot salad

This salad is a riot of color, with delicate flavors. The orange-blossom water gives it a mysterious perfume, but it is not an essential ingredient. Rose water is a good alternative.

2 oranges
2 cups (150g) radishes, trimmed
½ lb (200g) carrots, coarsely grated
2 tablespoons chopped fresh mint and dill
1 teaspoon cumin seeds, toasted in a dry pan
2 tablespoons orange-blossom water (optional)
sea salt
Serves 4

Finely grate the zest of 1 orange. Thickly slice the oranges through the skin, then cut away the peel. Cut the orange flesh into chunks.

Put the orange zest, orange chunks, radishes, carrots, and herbs in a large serving bowl and mix together. Add the cumin seeds, orange-blossom water, if using; then season with salt. Serve immediately.

orange, radish, and carrot salad

peas steamed with lettuce

In classical French cuisine, peas are cooked in this lovely fashion, known as *étuvée*. The lettuce, which is full of water, is swiftly braised, releasing the water as steam to cook the peas, imparting a subtle flavor. This method can also be used to cook green beans, sugar snap peas, and snowpeas.

lettuce leaves to cover the base of the saucepan
1lb (300g) peas or beans
1 tablespoon butter
pinch of sea salt
Serves 4

Line the base of a medium saucepan with lettuce and sprinkle with 1 tablespoon of water. Cover and gently heat on low until the lettuce starts to wilt. Add the peas or beans, butter, and salt, then cover and steam until the peas are cooked, about 5 minutes. Transfer to a warm serving dish and serve immediately.

smoked eggplant with cucumber and herbs

Eggplant is like a sponge. It absorbs flavors, oils, and juice with vigor. If you roast an eggplant over a flame until it is charred and ashen, the smoke will be absorbed by the flesh of the eggplant as it cooks. Eggplants have been cooked this way in the Mideast, India, and Southeast Asia for centuries. This recipe has a Thai character to it.

1 large or 2 medium eggplant
1oz (25g) roasted peanuts, chopped
2in (5cm) piece cucumber, diced
1 tablespoon snipped fresh chives
2 tablespoons chopped fresh mint
1 fresh green chile, seeded and chopped (optional)
1 lemon grass stalk, finely sliced (optional)
2 kaffir lime leaves, finely shredded (optional)
2 tablespoons fresh lime juice
1 tablespoons light soy sauce
1 teaspoon superfine sugar
Serves 4

Push a fork into the stem of the eggplant and place the body of the vegetable directly over a high gas flame. Turn occasionally until completely soft and collapsed—the skin should be blackened to the point of ash in places, and steam should be escaping through the fork holes. Alternatively, put the eggplant on a grill rack and broil under a preheated hot broiler until blistered all over.

Transfer the eggplant to a plate and let it cool. When cool enough to handle, peel off the charred skin. Put the eggplant meat and the remaining ingredients in a large serving bowl and mix together. Serve.

smoked eggplant with cucumber and herbs

salsas and chutneys

balsamic grape salsa

Balsamic vinegar is made from grape must (unfermented juice), so the famous vinegar and the fruit are natural partners in this salsa. If your grapes are very sour, you may want to add a pinch or two of sugar. The sweet yet savory flavor sensation combines well with broiled fish, poultry, or cooked beans.

½ lb (200g grapes), seeded and chopped
1 large shallot, finely chopped
1 tablespoon chopped dill
1 tablespoon chopped parsley
1 tablespoon good balsamic vinegar
1 tablespoon extra virgin olive oil
sea salt and freshly ground black pepper

Combine all the ingredients in a bowl. Set aside to let the flavors develop, ideally for about 30 minutes.

seared peach salsa

Searing gives a faintly smoky flavor to this salsa and makes the peach juices run to create a spicy syrup. Nectarines can be used the same way, but they tend to cling to their stones, making it difficult to halve them. I like to add lots of hot chile in this salsa. Like other fruit salsas, it lends itself well to egg, cheese, and bean dishes, as well as fish.

2 peaches, halved and stoned
1 small red onion, finely chopped
2 tablespoons fresh mint leaves, finely chopped
2–3 small fresh green chiles, finely chopped
juice of 1 lime
sea salt

Makes about 1 cup (250ml)

Heat a non-stick stove-top grill pan over medium heat without oil. Put the peaches cut side down in the hot pan and cook until blackened underneath and slightly softened all over. Remove from the pan and let them cool.

When the peaches are cool enough to handle, peel and chop finely. Put the peach flesh into a serving bowl, add the remaining ingredients, and mix well. Set aside for about 30 minutes to develop the flavors.

corn and avocado salsa

If you grow your own corn on the cob, you can experience its true sweetness at first hand—for, once the corn is picked, the sugars start to convert to starch. Corn on the cob is hard to beat, especially with lashings of butter. The buttery quality of avocado gives it an affinity with corn. This salsa is excellent with eggs, cheese, or any bean dish.

1 ear fresh corn, kernels stripped
1 large ripe avocado, diced
juice of 1–2 limes
1 fresh red chile, minced
2 scallions, chopped
8–10 fresh basil leaves, shredded
1 teaspoon superfine sugar
sea salt

Makes about 2 cups (500ml)

Bring a small saucepan of water to a boil over medium heat. Add the corn kernels and blanch them for 2 minutes. Strain and cool the kernels under cold running water, then drain thoroughly.

Put the kernels in a serving bowl, add the remaining ingredients, and mix together. Serve immediately.

olive and herb paté

This pungent paté—halfway between a tapenade and a chermoula—has many uses. Spread some on a cracker with creamy cheese or basil and chile labne (see page 110). Stir it into bulgar wheat, hot couscous, or hot soup. Coat fish or vegetables with the mixture before roasting or grilling. You can vary the fresh herbs, spices, and types of olive.

6–8 black olives, stoned
2 tablespoons chopped fresh dill
2 tablespoons chopped fresh flat-leaf parsley leaves
1 teaspoon grated zest of orange, satsuma, or similar
1 garlic clove, sliced
1 teaspoon ground cumin
½ teaspoon smoked or ordinary paprika
pinch of sea salt

Makes about ½ cup (100ml)

Put all the ingredients in a mortar and, using a pestle, pound until a thick, fairly smooth paste forms. Alternatively, use a spice grinder.

Transfer the paté to a serving dish or store in a small airtight container in the refrigerator until ready to use. Use within 3 days.

tomato and cashew chutney

Fresh, fast, and spicy, this South Indian-style chutney is best eaten on the day it is made. Scoop up the smooth sauce with poppadoms or tortilla chips. Or pour it on boiled rice and vegetables for a simple supper with a kick.

1lb (300g) tomatoes, quartered
4 whole garlic cloves
1 tablespoon sunflower oil
1oz (25g) cashew nuts
1 tablespoon sesame seeds
1 teaspoon cumin seeds
2 dried chiles
1 tablespoon brown sugar
sea salt

Sauté the tomatoes and garlic in the oil briskly until slightly softened, then cool. In a separate dry pan, sauté the cashews, sesame, cumin, and chiles until the sesame seeds pop. Combine with the tomatoes and garlic in a blender with sugar and salt. Purée until smooth. Serve with freshly cooked poppadoms.

cilantro chutney (left), tomato and cashew chutney (center), and roasted chile jam (right)

cilantro chutney

In India, this fresh "chutney" is not a preserve, but a few pungent ingredients puréed together, making it more like a sauce or a dip. It can be eaten with chips, raw vegetables, or poppadoms. Try it over baked or boiled potatoes, or as an accompaniment to roast vegetables. Cilantro (coriander) is not to everyone's taste—but in this combination, it works in harmony with the other ingredients to produce an effect quite different from that of the herb on its own.

1 large handful of fresh cilantro, cleaned and
   picked through
½ cup (120ml) natural yogurt
1 garlic clove
1 x 1in (2cm) piece of fresh ginger, chopped
2 fresh green chiles, seeded and chopped
a squeeze of lemon
sea salt
Makes 1 cup (250 ml)

If the cilantro is young, use the tender stems as well as the leaves. Chop the cilantro coarsely, then put it in a blender, add the remaining ingredients, and process until smooth. Transfer to a bowl and serve. The chutney keeps in the refrigerator for up to 3 days.

roasted chile jam

This is real jam and makes an unusual gift. It is a good sweet chile all-rounder that makes a wonderful accompaniment to cheese. The weight of the peppers reduces by about one third once they have been seeded, roasted, and skinned—so, when you have completed this process, weigh the peppers. The weight of the prepared peppers should be matched with the same weight of sugar with pectin.

7lb (3kg) fresh bell peppers (capsicums), halved and seeded
10 hot or 20 mild fresh chiles, or to taste, halved and seeded
4½ lb (2kg) sugar with pectin
juice and grated zest of 2 limes

2 large cookie sheets
mason jars
a heavy-based stainless-steel preserving pan
Makes about 7 cups (1.75 litres)

Put a saucer in the refrigerator for testing the jam later. Put the peppers and chiles cut side down on a large cookie sheet, and broil under a preheated hot broiler until blackened and blistered all over. Alternatively, roast in a preheated oven at the highest setting. Transfer to a plastic bag or bowl, seal or cover, and let them sweat until cool enough to handle.

Reduce the oven temperature or preheat to 325°F (160°C) to sterilize the jars. Before you begin, make sure the jars and lids are both very clean. If you are using rubber seals, they must be new. Stand the jars on a cookie sheet lined with paper towels and put in the oven for 10 minutes. Pour boiling water over the lids and rubber seals, if using.

Skin the peppers and chop coarsely. Crush the roasted chiles—remove the skin if it has become papery. Put the peppers in a food processor and process until a coarse purée forms. Scoop the pepper pulp into the preserving pan, add the sugar, lime juice, and zest, then bring to a boil, stirring. It should come to a fierce boil, scaling the walls of the pan in an eruption of glossy bubbles. Keep stirring and let it rage on for 4 minutes. Reduce the heat and test it on your chilled saucer. If it has set, a few drops should form a wrinkly skin on top. If not, boil for slightly longer. If it still doesn't set, add more lime juice. Let the jam stand for a few minutes, then ladle it into the prepared jars, leaving a little space. Attach the lids tightly and turn the jars upside down once. Use when cool or within 2 years.

sweet things

apples with thyme and brandy cream

Apples and thyme make a handsome couple in this hot and heavenly dessert. The apples can be prepared ahead of time and left to soak in water with a dash of lemon or cider vinegar, ready to be cooked after the main course, but dry them well first. Serve the dessert on its own or with vanilla ice cream. It's nice cold, too; the sauce cools to a luscious, thick toffee.

¼ stick (25g) butter
2 large cooking apples, or 3–4 smaller ones, peeled, cored, and sliced into rings or crescents 2in (5 mm) thick
leaves stripped from 6–8 fresh thyme sprigs
4 tablespoons unrefined sugar
4 tablespoons brandy
4 tablespoons heavy cream or crème fraîche
Serves 4

Have 4 serving bowls ready in a warm oven. Melt the butter in a stove-top grill pan over medium heat and arrange a single layer of apples in the base (they will probably have to be cooked in batches). Sprinkle with thyme leaves and sauté until the apples are light golden underneath. Turn them over carefully with a spatula and sprinkle on the sugar. When the sugar melts, shake the pan to coat the apples with the caramel butter, then spoon into the warmed bowls.

Return the grill pan to the heat and pour in the brandy. When it bubbles, add the cream. When the cream is heated through, pour it on the apples and serve immediately.

rhubarb with ginger-spiked meringue

Sharp rhubarb is the perfect foil for the sweet marshmallow taste of meringue. Fresh ginger elevates it to a level of elegance. You can use any fruit in this recipe—apples, quinces, and tart fruits work best. Serve with a little crème fraîche or yogurt.

2lb (1kg) rhubarb, cut into chunks
4 tablespoons light brown sugar, or to taste
3 egg whites
6oz (180g) superfine sugar
1in (2cm) piece of fresh ginger, finely grated

a large ovenproof dish, buttered
Serves 4

Put the rhubarb in the prepared dish and toss with the light brown sugar. Roast in a preheated oven at 425°F (220°C) for about 20–30 minutes until the rhubarb is softened.

Reduce the oven temperature to 350°F (180°C). Put the egg whites into a spotlessly clean, greasefree bowl and, using an electric whisk or mixer, whisk until stiff. Whisk in the sugar, a spoonful at a time, then whisk in the ginger. Spread the meringue over the cooked rhubarb and bake in the preheated oven for 20 minutes until barely crisp and golden on top. Serve immediately.

rhubarb with ginger-spiked meringue

lavender scones

lavender scones

Use lavender sparingly in this recipe—too much and the scones will taste of grandmother's perfume. The herb can have soporific effects, but a cup of coffee should counteract that.

¾ cup (180ml) milk
4–6 fresh lavender sprigs or 1 tablespoon lavender flowers
1lb (250g) all-purpose flour
1 teaspoon baking powder
4 tablespoons superfine sugar
½ stick (50g) cold butter, cubed
clotted cream or extra thick cream and berry jam, to serve

a fluted cookie cutter
a large cookie sheet, dusted with flour
Makes 8 scones

Put the milk and lavender in a small saucepan and bring to a boil over low heat. Remove the saucepan from the heat and pour the hot milk into a heatproof pitcher or bowl. Let it cool.

Sift together flour, baking powder, and sugar into a large bowl. Add the butter and, using your fingertips, rub together until crumbly.

Strain the milk and gradually add it to the flour mixture to form a soft dough. Add a little more flour if the mixture is too sticky. Turn the dough out onto a lightly floured work surface and press it down gently into a slab, about 1in (2cm) thick. Cut out rounds with a fluted cookie cutter. (To make baby scones, press the dough into a ½ in (1cm) thick slab and use a small cookie cutter to make 16 scones.) Gently press together irregular scraps to use all the dough.

Put the scones onto the prepared baking sheet and bake in a preheated oven at 350°F (180°C) for 15–20 minutes until golden. Serve warm or cold with cream and jam.

plum and ginger crumble

Plums are particularly beautiful in a crumble, oozing pink caramel juices around the edges of a golden crust. Most orchard fruits work well in a crumble—try apples, cherries, peaches, apricots, and pears. Make up a big batch of the crumble mixture and store it in portions in the freezer.

CRUMBLE
⅓ cup (120g) flour
1 stick (90g) butter, cubed
¼ cup (90g) superfine sugar
2 tablespoons pinola
4 tablespoons (50g) crystallized ginger, chopped

FILLING
1lb (500g) plums, stoned and chopped
2–3 tablespoons brown sugar
ice cream, cream, crème fraîche, or yogurt, to serve

a large ovenproof dish
Serves 4

To make the crumble topping, put the flour and butter in a bowl and, using your fingertips, rub together until crumbly. Stir in the sugar, pinola, and ginger, and mix well.

Put the plums in a separate bowl, add the brown sugar, and stir until the plums are coated evenly. Pour the plums in a large ovenproof dish and spread the crumble topping over it. Bake in a preheated oven at 400°F (200°C) for 30 minutes until golden and bubbling around the edges. Serve with a scoop of ice cream or some cream.

sweet berry butter

When the first few ripe berries appear on the plant—barely enough to fill a teacup—make the most of them by creating this outrageous condiment. Spead it on french toast, hot pancakes or just plain toast for a wicked treat. It doesn't keep for long—not least because it's irresistible—but it freezes well.

½ cup (75g) edible berries, mashed (at room temperature)
¾ stick (75g) soft unsalted butter (at room temperature)
¾ cup (150g) confectioner's sugar
Makes about 1 cup (300g)

Put the berries and butter in a bowl and beat together with a wooden spoon. Gradually beat in the sugar until a homogenous mixture is formed. Do not overbeat. If the mixture appears to curdle, add more sugar. Chill in the refrigerator and use within 24 hours or freeze for up to 6 months.

frozen fruit milkshake

When there is a glut of fruit in the garden and you don't have time to cook and bottle it all fresh, freezing is a great solution. This is a way of using your frozen surplus to make a superb breakfast, a cooler on a hot afternoon or an after dinner treat.

1lb (500g) frozen fruit such as plums, apricots, nectarines, peaches, berries
1 cup (250ml) milk
1 teaspoon pure vanilla essence
2–3 tablespoons confectioner's sugar, or to taste
Serves 4

Thaw the fruit just enough to break it up, then put it in a blender with the remaining ingredients and process for 2 minutes until smooth. Serve.

chamomile sorbet

This is a light, snowy, refreshing confection with all the soothing properties of chamomile. Like the renowned chamomile tea, it promotes good digestion and calms the nerves. You could substitute any sweet garden herb such as lavender or lemon balm.

2–3 tablespoons dried chamomile flowers or
    a handful of fresh herb
¼ cup (50g) sugar
squeeze of lemon

an ice cream maker or a wide, shallow freezerproof container
Serves 4

Put the camomile flowers into a heatproof bowl and pour in 2 cups (500ml) boiling water. Let it steep for 5 minutes. Strain into a saucepan and heat gently. Add the sugar and a few drops of lemon juice, and stir until the sugar is dissolved. Pour into a container, cool, and chill in the refrigerator.

When chilled, pour into an ice cream maker and freeze according to the manufacturer's instructions. The sorbet is best used soon after making. If stored in the freezer, it may become very solid; thaw for several minutes before serving.

Alternatively, pour into a wide, shallow freezerproof container to a depth of ½–1in (1–2cm). Put into the freezer for 1 hour or until it begins to freeze around the edges. Using a fork, scrape ice crystals away from the sides of the container and beat well. Freeze again for 30 minutes, then repeat the scraping and beating process until the mixture is a mass of fine crystals.

Another, simpler alternative is to freeze the sorbet in popsicle molds.

chamomile sorbet and frozen fruit milkshake

edibles for special purposes

The edible plants listed below are designed to give you ideas for your own kitchen garden. These lists are not intended to be comprehensive, but they identify herbs, vegetables, and fruit that are particularly suitable for growing in containers or in shady positions, as well as those that require minimal maintenance, and those that produce good crops in small spaces.

Containers If you work hard at it, you can grow almost anything in a container, but in practical terms it is sensible not to be too ambitious. A larger growing edible will require either a very substantial pot or constant watering in the season. Most plants that grow happily in containers will also grow on a roof garden, but they need protection from the extreme conditions, especially the wind. Provide shelter if possible. In a very windy area, choose dwarf varieties. Plants in containers need regular watering.

Allium sativum **Garlic**

Allium schoenoprasum **Chive**

Anethum graveolens **Dill**

Artemisia dracunculus **Tarragon**

Beta vulgaris **Beet** (globe types)

Beta vulgaris Cicla Group **Swiss chard**

Brassica oleracea Capitata Group **Cabbage** (miniature forms)

Capsicum annuum Grossum Group **Sweet pepper**

Capsicum annuum Longum Group **Chile**

Citrus spp. **Citrus fruits** (need protection)

Coriandrum sativum **Coriander (Cilantro)**

Cucumis sativus **Cucumber** (needs lots of watering and shelter from winds)

Cucurbita pepo **Zucchini** (needs large pot or barrel)

Daucus carota **Carrot** (short and round types)

Eruca vesicaria **Arugula**

Ficus carica **Fig** (needs large pot or barrel)

Fragaria spp. **Strawberry**

Latuca sativa **Lettuce**

Laurus nobilis **Bay**

Lavandula spp. **Lavender** (particularly cut and come again)

Lycopersicon esculentum **Tomato**

Malus sylvestris var. *domestica* on dwarf stock **Apple**

Mentha **Mint**

Ocimum basilicum **Basil**

Origanum spp. **Marjoram**

Petroselinum crispum **Parsley**

Phaseolus coccineus **Runner bean** (dwarf varieties easiest, though climbers are fine with enough water and shelter)

Phaseolus vulgaris **Snap bean** (dwarf varieties easiest, though climbers are fine with enough water)

Prunus persica **Peach** and **nectarine**

Pyrus communis var. *sativa* **Pear**

Raphanus sativus **Radish**

Rosmarinus officinalis **Rosemary**

Salvia officinalis **Sage**

Solanum melongena **Eggplant**

Solanum tuberosum **Potato** (new early)

Thymus spp. **Thyme**

Vaccineum corymbosum **Blueberry**

Vitis vinifera **Grapevine** (needs large pot or barrel)

Shade Few edibles will grow in deepest shade, though some can tolerate light to medium shade in a border or in a north-facing garden. However, many of these would be happier with a bit more sun.

Allium schoenoprasum **Chive**

Anthriscus cerefolium **Chervil**

Beta vulgaris **Beet**

Beta vulgaris **Chard**

Brassica oleracea Acephala Group **Kale**

Eruca vesicaria **Arugula**

Latuca sativa **Lettuce**

Laurus nobilis **Bay**

Mentha spp. **Mint**

Petroselinum crispum **Parsley**

Phaseolus coccineus **Runner bean**

Prunus cerasus **Morello cherry**

Raphanus sativus **Radish**

Rheum x *cultorum* **Rhubarb**

Ribes nigrum **Black currant**

Ribes uva-crispa **Gooseberry** (for cooking)

Rubus fruticosus **Blackberry**

Rumex acetosa **Sorrel**

Solanum tuberosum **Potato**

Spinacia oleracea **Spinach**

Lowest maintenance These edibles virtually look after themselves once they have been planted, provided that they are protected when young from slugs and snails.

Allium cepa Aggregatum Group **Shallot**

Allium porrum **Leek**

Allium sativum **Garlic**

Allium schoenoprasum **Chive**

Anethum graveolens **Dill**

Beta vulgaris **Beet**

Beta vulgaris Cicla Group **Chard**

Cynara scolymus **Globe artichoke**

Ficus carica **Fig**

Foeniculum vulgare **Fennel**

Fragaria vesca 'Semperflorens' **Alpine strawberry**

Laurus nobilis **Bay**

Lavandula spp. **Lavender**

Mentha **Mint**

Phaseolus coccineus **Runner bean**

Phaseolus vulgaris **Snap bean**

Rheum x *cultorum* **Rhubarb**

Rosmarinus spp. **Rosemary**

Rubus fruticosus **Blackberry**

Rubus idaeus **Raspberry**

Salvia officinalis **Sage**

Thymus spp. **Thyme**

Best croppers in small spaces This list covers edibles suitable for balconies and those that thrive when interspersed with ornamentals in a small garden. The herbs may not produce an enormous amount, but in many cases it takes only a small quantity of a herb to have a profound effect on a dish. Most herbs can be harvested through the season.

Allium cepa Aggregatum Group **Shallot**

Allium sativum **Garlic**

Allium schoenoprasum **Chive**

Anethum graveolens **Dill**

Artemisia dracunculus **Tarragon**

Beta vulgaris **Beet**

Beta vulgaris Cicla Group **Chard**

Capsicum annuum Longum Group **Chile**

Coriandrum sativum **Coriander (Cilantro)**

Daucus carota **Carrot**

Eruca vesicaria **Arugula**

Fragaria spp. **Strawberry**

Latuca sativa **Lettuce**

Laurus nobilis **Bay** (kept clipped and compact)

Lycopersicon esculentum **Tomato**

Ocimum basilicum **Basil**

Origanum spp. **Oregano** and **marjoram**

Petroselinum crispum **Parsley**

Phaseolus vulgaris **Snap bean**

Phaseolus coccineus **Runner bean**

Rosmarinus officinalis **Rosemary**

Rumex acetosa **Sorrel**

Salvia officinalis **Sage**

Satureja spp. **Savory**

Thymus **Thyme**

picture credits

All gardening photography by Caroline Hughes unless otherwise stated.
Food photography by William Shaw.

Key: ph=photographer, a=above, b=below, r=right, l=left, c=center.

1 Williams family garden, London; 2 Jane & George Nissen's house in London; 4a Adam Caplin's garden in north London; 4br Williams family garden, London; 6l Adam Caplin's garden in north London; 6r Francine Watson Coleman's organic garden in London; 7c & 8ac Jane & George Nissen's house in London; 8bl The Kitchen Garden in Troston, Suffolk; 8br Williams family garden, London; 9ac, 9ar & 9bcr The Kitchen Garden in Troston, Suffolk; 9bl Iden Croft Herbs; 9br HDRA's Yalding Organic Gardens, near Maidstone, Kent; 10c The Kitchen Garden in Troston, Suffolk; 10–11 & 11b Iden Croft Herbs; 11a Williams family garden, London; 12a & 13c June Brandon, Site Secretary, Barrowell Green Allotments, north London; 13r Jillian & Geoffrey Smith's garden in south-east London; 14b HDRA's Yalding Organic Gardens, near Maidstone, Kent; 14a Francine Watson Coleman's organic garden in London; 15r Adam Caplin's garden in north London; 16 HDRA's Yalding Organic Gardens, near Maidstone, Kent; 17l The Kitchen Garden in Troston, Suffolk; 17r Francine Watson Coleman's organic garden in London; 18c Jillian & Geoffrey Smith's garden in south-east London; 18–19 Jane & George Nissen's house in London; 20l Iden Croft Herbs; 21 Francine Watson Coleman's organic garden in London; 22–23 John and Joan Ward's garden in London; 23l Adam Caplin's garden in north London; 23r Francine Watson Coleman's organic garden in London; 24l Adam Caplin's garden in north London; 24ar Francine Watson Coleman's organic garden in London; 26a Williams family garden, London; 26b Iden Croft Herbs; 27l & 28a Titsey Place Gardens, Oxted, Surrey RH8 0SD; 28–29 & 29 John and Joan Ward's garden in London; 30al Francine Watson Coleman's organic garden in London, 30bl HDRA's Yalding Organic Gardens, near Maidstone, Kent; 30ar Titsey Place Gardens, Oxted, Surrey RH8 0SD; 30br June Brandon, Site Secretary, Barrowell Green Allotments, north London; 31a Francine Watson Coleman's organic garden in London; 31b, 33c & 34ac Williams family garden, London; 34bl John and Joan Ward's garden in London; 34–35a June Brandon, Site Secretary, Barrowell Green Allotments, north London; 35al The Kitchen Garden in Troston, Suffolk; 35ar & br Williams family garden, London; 35bl HDRA's Yalding Organic Gardens, near Maidstone, Kent; 40–41b & 43ar Iden Croft Herbs; 43al Mr & Mrs Williams' garden in Eltham, London; 45ac HDRA's Yalding Organic Gardens, near Maidstone, Kent; 45bc Mr & Mrs Miller's garden in London; 47al Iden Croft Herbs; 48c June Brandon, Site Secretary, Barrowell Green Allotments, north London; 55 & 59al Francine Watson Coleman's organic garden in London; 62b The Kitchen Garden in Troston, Suffolk; 77b HDRA's Yalding Organic Gardens, near Maidstone, Kent; 85 Jane & George Nissen's house in London; 88 Titsey Place Gardens, Oxted, Surrey RH8 0SD; 89ar June Brandon, Site Secretary, Barrowell Green Allotments, north London; 94bl Titsey Place Gardens, Oxted, Surrey RH8 0SD; 96bl Jillian & Geoffrey Smith's garden in south-east London; 97bl Jane & George Nissen's house in London; 99bc The Kitchen Garden in Troston, Suffolk; 102b ph Debi Treloar; 103 Titsey Place Gardens, Oxted, Surrey RH8 0SD; 136 Jillian & Geoffrey Smith's garden in south-east London; 139 Williams family garden, London.

The publishers would like to thank the following organizations for providing information and photographic locations:

Ash Green Organic Foods
The Den Farm, Den Farm Lane, Collier Street, Tonbridge, Kent TN12 9PX, UK (+44 1892 730 738)
Home and wholesale delivery service for Kent. Producers of organic apples. Produce sold at Sevenoaks market (Wed), Greenwich market (Sat), and Old Spitalfields (Sun).

HDRA (Henry Doubleday Research Association)
Ryton Organic Gardens, Coventry CV8 3LG, UK (+44 24 7630 3517; www.hdra.org.uk)
and Yalding Organic Gardens, Benover Road, Yalding, near Maidstone, Kent ME18 6EX, UK (+44 1622 814650)
Registered charity researching and promoting organic gardening, farming and food. Produces fact sheets and booklets on organic pest and disease control, fruit-tree management, weed control, and general organic gardening techniques. Please telephone for information.
Pages 9br, 14b, 16, 30bl, 35bl, 45ac, 77b.

Iden Croft Herbs
Frittenden Road, Staplehurst, Tonbridge, Kent TN12 0DH, UK (+44 1580 891432; www.herbs-uk.com)
Pages 9bl, 10–11, 11b, 20l, 26b, 40–41b, 43ar, 47al.

The Kitchen Garden
Church Lane, Troston, Bury St Edmunds, Suffolk IP31 1EX, UK (+44 1359 268 322; www.kitchen-garden-hens.co.uk)
Small shop selling perennial and vegetable plants and specializing in nice things for gardeners.
Pages 8bl, 9ac, 9ar, 9bcr, 10c, 17l, 35al, 62b, 99bc.

Titsey Place Gardens
Oxted, Surrey RH8 0SD, UK (+44 1273 407056)
Please telephone for information.
Pages 27l, 28a, 30ar, 88, 94bl, 103.

resources

The following organizations will supply seeds and plants for the new kitchen garden.

The Banana Tree Inc.
715 Northampton Street
Easton, PA 18042
(610) 253-9589
www.banana-tree.com
Specialist in tropical fruits.

W. Atlee Burpee Seed Co.
300 Park Avenue
Warminster, PA 18974
(800) 888-1447
www.burpee.com
Seeds for vegetables and herbs.

Carroll Gardens
444 E. Main Street
Westminster, MD 21157
(800) 638-6334
www.carrollgardens.com
Herb plants, including tricolor sage.

Companion Plants
7247 N. Collville Ridge Road
Athens, OH 45701
(740) 592-4643
www.companionplants.com
Herbs, seeds, and roots.

The Cook's Garden
P.O. Box 535
Londonderry, VT 05148
(800) 547-9703
www.cooksgarden.com
Seeds include 'Lollo Rossa' and other cut-and-come-again lettuces.

DeBaggio Herbs
43494 Mountain View Drive
Chantilly, VA 20152
(703) 327-6976
www.debaggioherbs.com
Herbs and vegetables.

Glasshouse Works
P.O. Box 97, Church Street
Stewart, OH 45778
(800) 837-2142
www.rareplants.com
Herbs and other ornamental plants.

Goodwin Creek Gardens
P.O. Box 83
Williams, OR 97544
(800) 846-7359
www.goodwincreekgardens.com
Medicinal and culinary herbs.

The Gourmet Gardener
12287 117th Drive
Live Oak, FL 32060
(888) 404-4769
www.gourmetgardener.com
An international collection of seeds.

Gurney's Seed & Nursery Co.
110 Capitol St.
Yankton, SD 57079
(800) 806-1972
www.gurneys.com
Many fruit trees, including "pole-style" apple trees.

Harris Seeds
355 Paul Road
P.O. Box 24966
Rochester, NY 14624
(800) 514-4441
www.harrisseeds.com
Good selection of vegetable seeds.

Mellinger's Inc.
2310 W. South Range Road
North Lima, OH 44452
(800) 321-7444
www.mellingers.com
Tree fruit, berries, and grapes.

Nichols Garden Nursery
1190 Old Salem Road, NE
Albany, OR 97321
(541) 928-9280
www.nicholsgardennursery.com
Seeds for herbs and vegetables.

Nourse Farms
41 River Road
South Deerfield, MA 01373
(413) 665-2658
www.noursefarms.com
Strawberries, raspberries, blueberries, blackberries, rhubarb, asparagus.

Park Seed
1 Parkton Avenue
Greenwood, SC 29647
(800) 845-3369
www.parkseed.com
Seeds, fruits, and berries.

Peaceful Valley Farm Supply
P.O. Box 2209
Grass Valley, CA 95945
(888) 784-1722
www.groworganic.com
Seeds and cover crops, seed-starting supplies, cold frames, pest controls.

Piedmont Plant Company
807 N. Washington Street
P.O. Box 424
Albany, GA 31702
(800) 541-5185
www.plantfields.com
Vegetables and herbs.

Redwood City Seed Company
Box 361
Redwood City, CA 94064
(650) 325-7333
www.redwoodcityseed.com
Seeds for heirloom vegetables, hot peppers, and herbs.

Seeds of Change
P.O. Box 15700
Santa Fe, NM 87506
(888) 762-7333
www.seedsofchange.com
Organic seeds.

Stokes
P.O. Box 548
Buffalo, NY 14240
(800) 396-9238
www.stokeseeds.com
Seeds for herbs and vegetables.

The Thyme Garden
20546 Alsea Highway
Alsea, OR 97324
(541) 487-8671
www.thymegarden.com
A comprehensive collection of thyme and other herbs.

Tomato Grower's Supply Company
P.O. Box 2237
Fort Myers, FL 33902
(888) 478-7333
www.tomatogrowers.com
Seeds for tomatoes and peppers.

Wayside Gardens
1 Garden Lane
Hodges, SC 29695-0001
(800) 845-1124
www.waysidegardens.com
Fruit trees and vines.

White Flower Farm
P.O. Box 50
Litchfield, CT 06759
(800) 503-9624
www.whiteflowerfarm.com
Kitchen garden seeds.

Index

Figures in *italics* indicate captions; figures in **bold** indicate main entries.

RECIPES

acknowledgments

Adam Caplin:
I would like to thank Caroline Hughes for her wonderful photographs and
location hunting, and her great eye. I enjoyed every moment of our time together.

Thanks to all at Ryland Peters & Small, particularly Henrietta Heald for being a wonderful editor
and for being supportive and patient beyond the call of duty; Sally Powell for the marvelous design
of the book; Kate Blunt, Sarah Hepworth, Emily Westlake, Elizabeth of Mar, Joanna Everard,
Alison Starling, and Gabriella Le Grazie for helping to produce a book that I'm proud of.
Thank you to my agent Fiona Lindsay for her support and understanding.

Thanks also to all the garden owners who allowed us into their gardens and gave me
some invaluable practical horticultural advice: Francine Raymond, June Brandon,
Francine Watson Coleman, Jane and George Nissen, Jillian and Geoffrey Smith,
Joan and John Ward, Mr and Mrs Miller, and Rosemary Titterington.

Special thank yous go to Nick Robinson for being such a great help, all at HDRA,
Barry Holdsworth for his generosity and expertise, and Ken Black for sharing his extraordinary
knowledge. Thanks also to Carolyn Hutchinson, Caroline Foley, and Stephanie Donaldson
for their help, friendship, and support.

Caroline Hughes:
I would like to thank all the team at Ryland Peters & Small, particularly Gabriella Le Grazie,
Sally Powell, and Alison Starling—it has been a real joy to work on this book.

A huge thank you to Adam Caplin for making it such fun to collaborate with
him—his wit and wisdom were much appreciated.

Heartfelt thanks to all those who were kind enough to give time, advice, and access
to their beautiful gardens. Special mentions are due to Barry Holdsworth and the staff at
Titsey Place, Nick and the staff at Yalding Organic Garden, Jillian and Geoffrey Smith,
and to Mat for the ideas and inspiration.

Celia Brooks Brown:
Heartfelt thanks to Anya and Jonathan Finney for letting me potter around their
magnificent garden and kitchen during the development and writing of the recipes.
Thanks to Fiona Smith and William Shaw for bringing them to life on these pages,
and to Henrietta Heald for her wonderful placidity.

root vegetables

Root vegetables are a magical addition to the garden—partly because of the mystery of the crop that lies underneath the soil. The childlike expectation associated with pulling carrots, seeing the shape and size of a new parsnip, or digging up and counting a crop of succulent new potatoes introduces a new dimension to growing edibles.

Root vegetables prefer well-drained soil with few stones that has been enriched the previous year with manure—apart from potatoes, which appreciate manure at any time. Most prefer sun. They resent being moved and are best sown in position unless they have been started in biodegradable containers.

Beta vulgaris. **Beet**. Beets have bold leaves and come not only in red but also in yellow or white, and even with striped flesh. 'Bull's Blood' is the most vibrant, with burgundy foliage that looks great when planted in a group, contrasting with other leaf shades. The globe types grow well in pots. Sow bolt-resistant varieties outdoors from early spring. Young leaves are lovely in salads; older ones can be cooked as greens.

Brassica napus Napobrassica Group. **Rutabaga**. Rutabaga is not very ornamental. It prefers cool, damp conditions. Sow disease-resistant seed outside in early summer and harvest from fall onwards. Keep well watered to aid growth and to help control flea beetle.

Brassica rapa Rapifera Group. **Turnip**. Turnip grows fast—some mature in about 60 days—and comes in designer ranges, but is not very ornamental. Turnip can take a little shade and likes cool damp conditions. Grow as rutabaga. Harvest entire crop in fall before they go woody, and store.

Daucus carota. **Carrot**. With its attractive feathery leaves, carrot looks good as spot planting in gaps or in clumps, particularly near other fine

canes or along string suspended from overhead wires. This s
artistry adds a new vertical dimension to a garden and, like a
sculpture, changes over time.

Among other vegetables that make excellent vertical highli
squashes and gourds, cucumber, and peas. More vigorous vari
gourds can get quite heavy and are likely to need more substar

Feeding Provided that the soil is healthy and appropriate for th
little regular feeding is required for crops in the ground. Adding
and manure will provide them with most of their vital nutrients.
main nutrients needed are nitrogen (N) for leaf growth, phospho
for root growth, and potassium (K) for flowering and fruiting. Lo
fertilizers that have been formulated to promote the type of crop

FAR LEFT **Beets should be lifte
a gentle tug and a twist—the
are also edible.**

LEFT **A lettuce as large and spl
as this 'Verde d'Inverno' calls f
leisurely alfresco meal with frie**

BELOW LEFT AND RIGHT **A newly
harvested parsnip is a reminder
the hidden world beneath the s
Garlic pulled in late summer can
stored for ages in a cool dry plac**

want: high nitrogen for leafy crops, high phosphates for roots, and high
potassium for fruiting crops. Plants in containers will need more regular
feeding—and the same rule applies.

Rotation Because vegetables have specific soil and mineral requirements,
they should be grown in different places in the garden from year to year
– a technique called rotation. This is particularly important in the case
of brassicas, which are vulnerable to club root, an extremely debilitating
fungal disease that can easily build up in the soil.

Pests and diseases There are many pests and diseases that affect
vegetables, although many of these are kept at a manageable level in
the mixed garden. The more intensive your planting becomes, the
more work and knowledge is required to prevent a small and harmless
infection becoming a more difficult problem.

OPPOSITE, LEFT AND RIGHT **Beets are attractive foliage plants that look especially effective in a group. I like the red etching that seems to flow from the base.**

LEFT AND FAR LEFT **The whispering leaves of carrot help to lighten an area, and the short-rooted varieties are easy to grow in containers.**

BELOW **Parsnip is one of those vegetables in which the prize below the soil is more interesting than the architecture above.**

foliage such as achillea and nigella. The miniature and short-rooted varieties are good in containers. Sow early types in spring followed by a main crop in early summer. Growing in a mixed garden helps to reduce risk of attack by carrot fly. Planting near onions also helps. If it is left to grow for a second year, carrot produces attractive flowers, which appeal to beneficial insects.

Helianthus tuberosus. **Jerusalem artichoke**. Perennial. Jerusalem artichoke grows up to 10ft (3m) tall with sage-green leaves. It makes a useful screening plant, providing shelter from the wind and blocking out undesirable views. Can be used as a living frame for annual climbers such as sweet peas or the lovely yellow-flowered canary creeper. Slightly more compact varieties are available. 'Fuseau' is particularly good for cooking. The flowers resemble small sunflowers in late summer. Plant tubers about 6in (15cm) deep in mid spring. Stake taller varieties if in a windy spot, and start to harvest in fall when leaves turn brown.

Pastinaca sativa. **Parsnip**. Parsnip is not particularly ornamental unless left for a second year, when it produces an enormous head of seeds and flowers, which attract insects. Sow seed in late spring, three seeds to a planting hole, and thin out weaker seedlings. In a mixed, border grow shorter-rooted varieties, which can be harvested without too much disturbance.

Raphanus sativus. **Radish**. Radish is quick to grow but not as easy as people think. The plants themselves are not especially attractive, although letting some go to seed is worthwhile. Sow in any soil from spring to early fall in sun or dappled shade. Podding radishes such as 'Munchen Bier' combine beautiful flowers with unusual edible pods.

Solanum tuberosum. **Potato**. Try a few 'earlies', which will thrive in a barrel or in a small space in the garden—the foliage is a restful green and the taste bears no comparison to supermarket potatoes. The early potatoes grow fast and are less prone than the maincrops to pests and diseases. Start potatoes into growth in early spring by laying tubers in a shallow tray in light dry conditions, with the eyes uppermost. Plant when the sprouts are about 1in (2cm) long. Potato is a heavy feeder, so add plenty of rich organic matter and manure to the soil. Plant about 6in (15cm) deep and 1ft (30cm) apart. As the shoots grow, keep earthing them up to encourage more tubers and prevent greening. Potato is ready to harvest when in flower. Varieties such as 'Swift' and 'Rocket' are fun to grow in large containers.

ABOVE **Radishes take only a short time to mature and have a reputation for being one of the easiest vegetables to grow, but they can disappoint.**

LEFT **Although the potato may be an uninspiring plant in isolation, there is something wholesome and earthy about having potatoes in your garden, where they add the sense of satisfaction associated with being a provider.**

ABOVE **The magic of the harvest is never better captured than in the discovery of a potato crop under the soil. You may sometimes find a good crop spreading out a surprising distance from the plant.**